To Tom,
Happy Father's Day,
Love,
Pat
6/12

The Book of SPAM®

The Book of SPAM®

A Most Glorious and Definitive Compendium

of the World's Favorite Canned Meat

by

Dan Armstrong and Dustin Black

ATRIA BOOKS

New York · London · Toronto · Sydney

ATRIA BOOKS

A Division of Simon & Schuster, Inc.
1230 Avenue of the Americas
New York, NY 10020

First Atria Books hardcover edition August 2007

ATRIA BOOKS and colophon are trademarks of Simon & Schuster, Inc.

SPAM and all SPAM-derived terms are registered trademarks of Hormel Foods, LLC,
and are used with permission from Hormel Food Corporation.

For information about special discounts for bulk purchases,
please contact Simon & Schuster Special Sales at
1-800-456-6798 or business@simonandschuster.com.

Manufactured in the United States of America

1   3   5   7   9   10   8   6   4   2

ISBN-13: 978-0-7432-9192-7
ISBN-10:   0-7432-9192-1

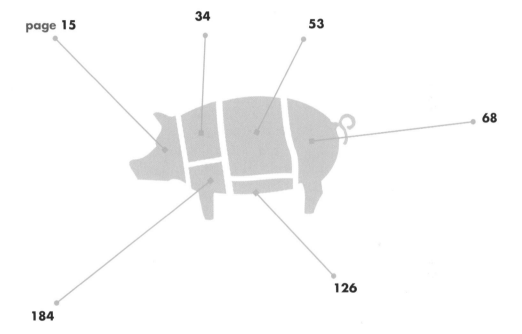

WHAT'S INSIDE:
the Table of Contents

WHY IS SPAM SO UNBELIEVABLY AWESOME?

To many, if not most, SPAM is an enigma wrapped in a secret with a side of confusion. It brings a smile to countless faces. It is loved by millions around the world. SPAM can be found almost anywhere. Almost everyone on the planet recognizes the name and the product. But it has remained widely misunderstood. Heck, many people think it's got something to do with email. It's enough to break your heart. But despite all that, it remains so fantastically SPAM-like. What gives?

I ♥ SPAM

Why is SPAM so lovable?

Sure, it's freaking delicious. That goes without saying. There are countless, amazing ways you can serve SPAM. It lasts forever, on your shelf and in your soul. There is the simple fact that SPAM is fun. It is a product that doesn't take itself too seriously, but still delivers when it counts. It represents all things American and patriotic. It's a fun word to say. It's even a fun word to look at.

All of these things add up to something bigger. Something that truly inspires people. The SPAM world is growing every day. Eventually it will be bigger than the universe. Get used to it. It's going to be meat-tastical.

FIND THE CAN OF SPAM.

Do you think it is easy to find the SPAM? Do not kid yourself. Do you see SPAM now, over there, by the tree? What you don't know is that SPAM was there only for an instant. You see, this is a photograph taken in the past. Only a photograph from the future could truly reveal where SPAM is now.

This decorative wall hanging reveals through metaphor that to SPAM, the world is simply a party favor.

His license plate tells us one thing, but his shirt tells us something different.

The first documented use of SPAM therapy. The patient's mood was quite positively impacted.

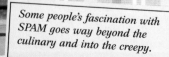

Some people's fascination with SPAM goes way beyond the culinary and into the creepy.

Mr. Cornwall's SPAM Haiku

This is not the SPAM asking you to send money to Nigeria.

Deep in the eye of SPAM there is a meat storm.

"Enjoy your 'outside time' this year, kids. Then it's back to the basement to crank out more of Dad's hippie tees."

WHAT IS SPAM?

This is the age-old question. There are many myths about what goes into our most beloved pork treat. We hate to have to repeat all the vicious slander and defamation of the good character of the precious SPAM, but we see it as our duty. Only through examining these lies can the truth be reached.

Early ads like this one mislead consumers to believe that SPAM was made by tiny elderly elves.

What is SPAM?

"Whatever it is, it's not meat." Nothing could be further from the truth. Hormel Foods is filled with honest, hardworking men and women who would never short-shrift the SPAM-loving public. Those kinds of shenanigans don't get past the Food and Drug Administration. The FDA makes sure that everybody who sells meat is selling actual meat. SPAM is no exception.

"Lips and A**holes." Absolutely not. These parts are not used for anything. Ick! Besides being totally illegal, who would be evil enough to try and feed that to someone? Last we checked, Satan does not work at Hormel Foods.

"It comes from the SPAMINAL™." This is really cute. Do you see what they did? They took two words (in this case "SPAM" and "animal") and smushed them together in a lame attempt at some kind of crass humor. "Look, it makes a new word. Aren't I funny?" says this person to himself. No, there is no such thing as a SPAMINAL. But it would be a cool prison nickname, if you get to choose one. Fingers crossed!

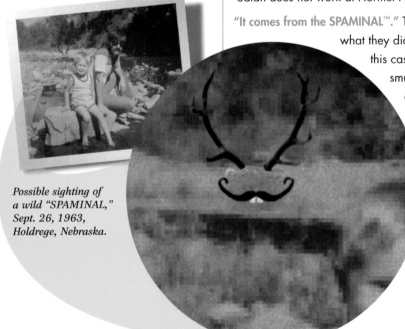

Possible sighting of a wild "SPAMINAL," Sept. 26, 1963, Holdrege, Nebraska.

The old joke was they used every part of the pig—except the squeal. That changed in the 1930s when Hormel launched their corporate newsletter "The Squeal." It was then that every last part of the pig was officially used.

Who knew?

No, really, what is SPAM?

"Everything scraped off the floor and all the other useless bits." No way. First off, there is no such thing as a "useless bit" of a pig. Everything is used, even the squeal. Secondly, if you're talking about floor scrapings, you've got SPAM confused with some super-evil hot-dog factory that exists only in our imaginations. Floor scrapings are either thrown away or fed to other animals. But never, ever used in SPAM.

"It's made from squirrels, possums, and other such furry creatures." While these woodland buddies may be eaten, and were certainly dinner during pioneer times, there just isn't enough meat on them to make them worth it. Plus, possums have naked tails. What's up with that?

Ingredients: Pork with Ham, Salt, Water, Sugar, Sodium Nitrite.

NET WT 12 OZ (340g)

U.S. INSPECTED AND PASSED BY DEPARTMENT OF AGRICULTURE

SEE INSIDE LABEL

Hormel Foods

Serving Suggestion

Now we can tell you that SPAM contains some pretty high-quality ingredients. But would you believe it? Maybe it's a good thing that people aren't sure what's in there. Leaving it shrouded in darkness makes it seem dangerous and extra sexy. However, this is a book about SPAM. We all know that such a book must serve truth and light.

The real answer lies in the most unexpected place, the label.

Many cultures eat all kinds of different meats. Some are downright gross. In a pinch, kangaroo meat may not be so bad. But SPAM® Classic is made from pigs, and only pigs. Damn if that ain't tasty.

1 2 Ingredients: 3 Pork with 4 Ham, Salt, 5 Water, Sugar, Sodium 6 Nitrite.

It's not magic, it's just good ingredients

Pork shoulder.  What is pork? Pork is from pigs. And a shoulder is a shoulder. This meat is usually a bit more fatty than other cuts, which makes it juicy and tender and adds more flavor. Aren't animals delicious?

Ham. Yet again, this one is pretty simple. Much like the pork shoulder, the ham is a cut of pork—but from the opposite end of the pig. ② Specifically, from the rear thigh. This is the same delicious treat served at Christmas dinner or Easter brunch or during reruns of *MacGyver*.

Salt. Good old sodium chloride. ③ Salt is pretty standard. Not sure we can even make a joke here. Sorry.

I'm learning!

SPAM comes from pigs because they are made of meat. Delicious, delicious meat.

Water. Again, nothing special here. ④ Plain, everyday H_2O is used in just about everything.

$NaNO_2$ turns yuck into yummy!

Sugar. ⑤ Yep. Not very scary so far, is it?

Sodium nitrite. ⑥ OK, this one might sound scary. But sodium nitrite is found in many foodstuffs. Salami, hot dogs, pepperoni, bologna, ham, bacon, and SPAM all contain very small amounts of sodium nitrite. Why? Sodium nitrite helps to preserve the pink color of SPAM. People do not like gray meat. Also, sodium nitrite helps to prevent botulism. Food poisoning is nasty. Have you ever had it?

Water

SUGAR

All pigs want to become SPAM. But Pig #79-8AU is trying much harder than the rest to make her dreams come true!

1937–2001

For the love of God, someone remove that gel from this otherwise perfect product!
Can't you see it is disturbing this young lady?

The Gel: Why, God, why?

OK, obviously there's a 900-pound gorilla in the room that we're not talking about. To many people, it is the supreme reason they dislike SPAM. We are talking about the mystery gel, SPAM Jelly, or "that weird goop." Some people may think it's an ingredient, but the gel is a natural and harmless by-product of the cooking process.

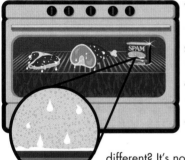

When you cook any meat, you expect some grease to come out, right? Hamburgers, steaks, pork chops, even filet mignon have some runoff. It's what adds extra sizzle to the pan. So why is SPAM any different? It's not. But since SPAM is cooked in the can, the gel has nowhere to run to.

The gel has sadly led many SPAM newcomers astray. It appears foreign and unnatural when in fact it is not. It's just the way it is, and there's nothing wrong with that. Just like it's good to cry sometimes. But not all the time, OK? You promised.

Many have washed their SPAM in the sink to remove the gel. Some have even experimented with it and came to realize it was a darn good furniture polish.

Well, whether you hate the gel or simply don't mind it, forget about it. It's gone.

No one misunderstood the gel as much as Judy.

Unauthorized Gel Uses

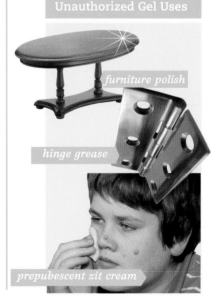

furniture polish

hinge grease

prepubescent zit cream

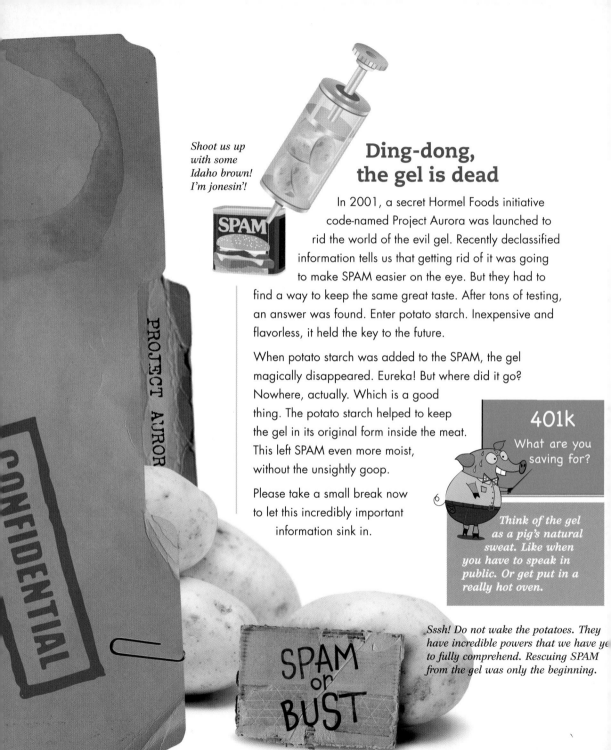

Shoot us up with some Idaho brown! I'm jonesin'!

Ding-dong, the gel is dead

In 2001, a secret Hormel Foods initiative code-named Project Aurora was launched to rid the world of the evil gel. Recently declassified information tells us that getting rid of it was going to make SPAM easier on the eye. But they had to find a way to keep the same great taste. After tons of testing, an answer was found. Enter potato starch. Inexpensive and flavorless, it held the key to the future.

When potato starch was added to the SPAM, the gel magically disappeared. Eureka! But where did it go? Nowhere, actually. Which is a good thing. The potato starch helped to keep the gel in its original form inside the meat. This left SPAM even more moist, without the unsightly goop.

Please take a small break now to let this incredibly important information sink in.

401k
What are you saving for?

Think of the gel as a pig's natural sweat. Like when you have to speak in public. Or get put in a really hot oven.

Sssh! Do not wake the potatoes. They have incredible powers that we have yet to fully comprehend. Rescuing SPAM from the gel was only the beginning.

PROJECT AUROR

CONFIDENTIAL

SPAM or BUST

2001–FOREVERMORE

Happiness and joy! Now that the gel is gone,
everything is right in the world. The sun shines and butterflies sing!

His backyard SPAM Museum may not have been a success, but his beard now has a cult following.

SO GOOD 1-800-LUV-SPAM™ IT'S GONE

SPAM™ FAN
www.spam.com

Sure, this frame was really expensive. But a glimpse of this man's posterior is priceless.

Neville's SPAM Haiku

A book about SPAM?
What kind of dumb crap is that?
Why did you buy it?

This rare SPAM trout swims upstream all year. But then it gets to make sweet, sweet fish love all night long. Then it dies.

Pigs have career day, too. Here's a SPAM recruiter hard at work.

Wearing a 40-pound SPAM hat could be vertebrae-crushing deadly. Who's the real SPAM fan now?

While having a SPAM wedding may seem a risky choice, it is much safer than the alternatives: Star Trek or totally nude.

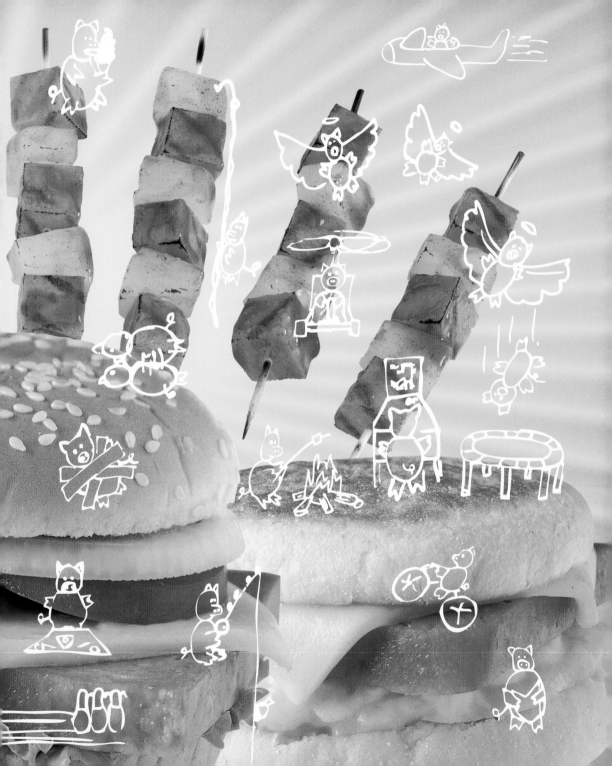

Never send a clown to do a journalist's job. While entertaining, Zippy's account of the manufacture of SPAM is highly inaccurate. To find out how SPAM is really made, turn the page.

Inside the SPAM plant

THE REAL DEAL

It begins when mountains of pork and ham are ground down.

As if that wasn't enough, then they kick in more stuff like salt and sugar. Just like a margarita after a Macarena marathon.

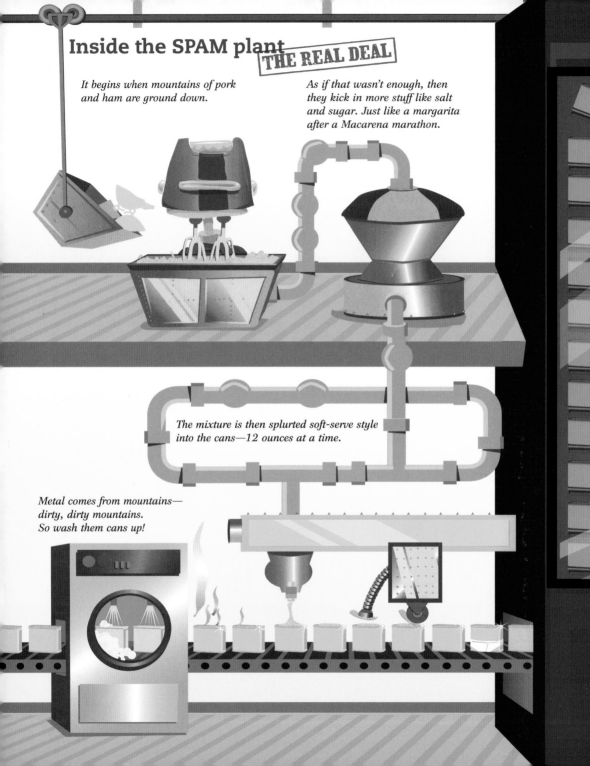

The mixture is then splurted soft-serve style into the cans—12 ounces at a time.

Metal comes from mountains— dirty, dirty mountains. So wash them cans up!

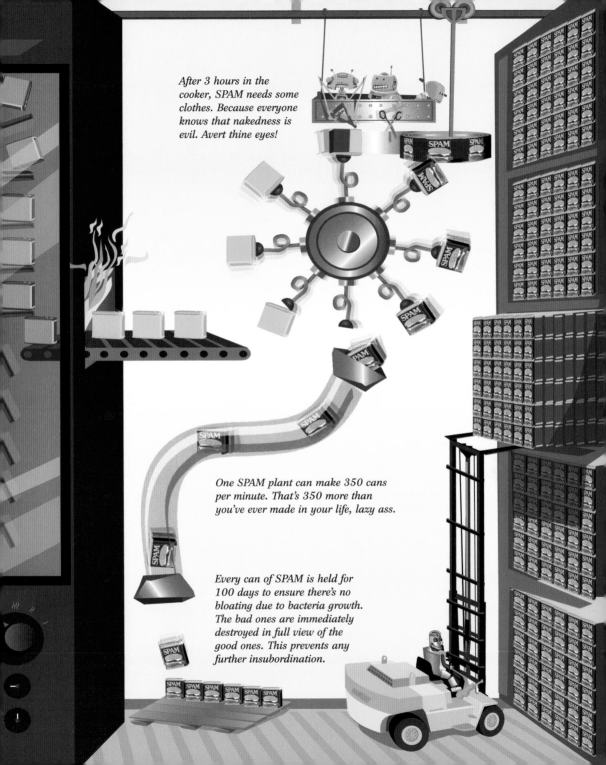

After 3 hours in the cooker, SPAM needs some clothes. Because everyone knows that nakedness is evil. Avert thine eyes!

One SPAM plant can make 350 cans per minute. That's 350 more than you've ever made in your life, lazy ass.

Every can of SPAM is held for 100 days to ensure there's no bloating due to bacteria growth. The bad ones are immediately destroyed in full view of the good ones. This prevents any further insubordination.

QUEST FOR SHELF LIFE

How did SPAM come to be? If you think about it, SPAM was inevitable. It was simply natural selection. Within SPAM can be found the apex of food preservation, the magnificence and portability of canning technology, the great human intuition that led to easy-open packaging, and the quintessence of flavor as sought with such difficulty from the four corners of the globe. The march of time brought us here, to SPAM. You'll see.

If only SPAM had been invented millions of years ago. Mankind would be so much farther along. We'd wear jetpacks and make tofu illegal.

You hungry. Pick berry to eat.

a)

b)

You survived all the dinosaurs and wild animals only to pick a poisonous berry.

Congrats. You picked a nutritious berry. Now start over.

Prehistoric times

The Quest for Shelf Life was a difficult task that began so long ago. Early man first gathered his food, picking berries and frolicking in the wilderness while avoiding toothy dinosaurs. Then came the discovery of pointed sticks and heavy rocks used to hunt the wonderful meat that was wandering about. This was awfully hard work.

Dinosaur friends are fun. Just always pretend to like their gifts!

Since the first day a caveman ate fresh meat, we have searched for a better way to preserve food. The lack of properly preserved food brought devastating famines and threatened our very existence. It confused early man and hurt his feelings deeply. Only with a secure reserve of nourishment could man turn his attention from hunting and gathering and begin to chase butterflies and write poems and develop $300 designer blue jeans.

Ug and his wife argue over who ate the last dried newt. She reminds him that they'd have more food if he didn't spend all their rock and stick currency on Brazilian waxes.

I, Beast Master

Animal husbandry to the rescue! Cows and pigs and goats and other delicious creations could be corralled and bred, keeping an easy and steady source of savory flavor nearby. But this was also kind of hard. The stupid animals needed a lot of attention and could not play checkers. Also, there was so much wasted meat because it could not all be eaten as fast as one would like.

Somehow, somewhere in Europe, sometime during the late 1400s or early 1500s, there came a new technique for preserving meat, pork in particular. It was called potting. Probably called that because they used clay pots? Totally guessing here.

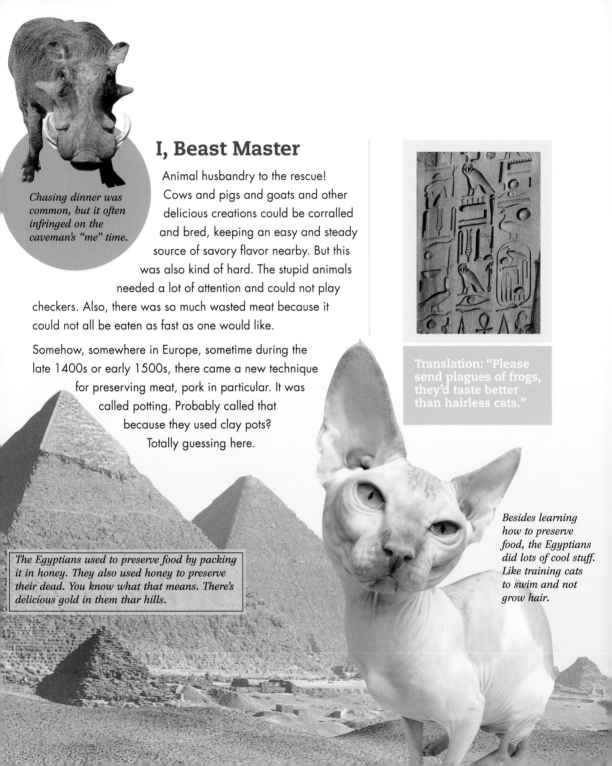

Chasing dinner was common, but it often infringed on the caveman's "me" time.

Translation: "Please send plagues of frogs, they'd taste better than hairless cats."

Besides learning how to preserve food, the Egyptians did lots of cool stuff. Like training cats to swim and not grow hair.

The Egyptians used to preserve food by packing it in honey. They also used honey to preserve their dead. You know what that means. There's delicious gold in them thar hills.

The era of potted meat

How does one pot meat? Well, in medieval times, an earthenware pot was filled with layers of cooked pork. While that pork was cooking, they saved the grease. That grease was then used to seal every layer of pork, protecting it from air and bacteria. Basically, you've got yourself a very rudimentary can of SPAM. Simply throw it in the cellar and grab delicious and juicy pieces of pork whenever you want. Hopefully, when it runs out, you've got another pig to slaughter. If not, you would be "scraping the bottom of the barrel."

Woe unto he who taketh the name of SPAM in vain.

Drying and salting meats had been around for a while. But it made the meat way too dry and way too salty. Without any cold beer around, who wants that? So potting meat became an early way to preserve the great pork flavor and moistocity.

HEREIN LAYETH THE JUISIESTE, MOSTE REGALE PORKE PRODUFTS KNOWNE ACROFT HIF MAGEFTYES EMPIRE

grease

pork

grease

pork

grease

Strawberry ice cream. No, just kidding, it's more pork.

grease

pork

grease

pork

grease

Teens out clubbing. Oh, how times have changed.

Luncheon Meat or Fancy French Food?
You be the Judge

SPAM VS. Rillettes

Anyone who has studied French cuisine should know what a rillette is.
Pork rillettes are basically the French cuisine version of SPAM. The French
have made so many huge advances in the world of food. They even came
close to the majesty of SPAM. Nice try, Pierre. Close, but no éclair.

HEY KIDS, HELP WILBUR FULFILL
HIS DESTINY

Wilbur is captured and has to play dress-up with an effeminate French boy. Bad touché!

Wilbur ends up in the zoo. It's not so bad, except for having to be Simba's roommate.

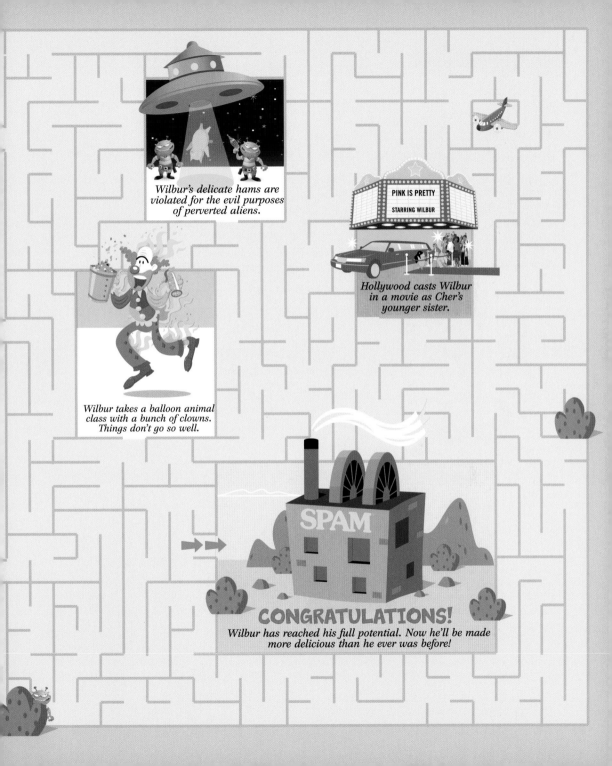

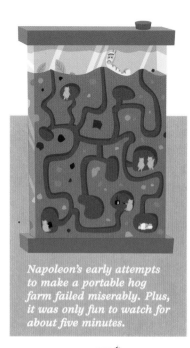

Napoleon's early attempts to make a portable hog farm failed miserably. Plus, it was only fun to watch for about five minutes.

Considering the tumultuous history of pig preservation, we should consider ourselves lucky that we live in an era of heightened can technology. What a suckfest the past would have been.

The French Revolution

OK, so potting meat solved the problem of saving the meat for a month or two, maybe even through a winter. But the earthenware pots were very delicate, and the whole system depended on cool temperatures, which meant keeping them in the cellar. This was simply not good enough. Man wanted to move. They had boats to explore the world with and armies to attack faraway lands, and these sailors and soldiers needed to pack a couple hundred thousand lunches. So what to do?

In 1795, Napoleon offered 12,000 francs to anyone who could come up with a food preservation technique to help feed his troops. That many francs was like a thousand billion dollars nowadays. But that's just how important it was to Napoleon at the time. He simply couldn't take over the world without some form of portable food.

With new food technology to feed his soldiers, Napoleon was able to focus on more pressing issues. Like fancy outfits.

Nick "The Jar" Appert, father of food preservation and the faux-hawk.

Luckily, a French brewer named Nicolas Appert had plenty of spare time. He began bottling partially cooked meat in wide-mouthed bottles, sealing them with cork, wiring them shut, and placing the bottles in boiling water for several hours. Without fully understanding the science behind it, Appert had stumbled on the perfect solution to Napoleon's problem.

Napoleon's military forces loved it and everyone smiled while they ate. Pre-cooked beef with gravy and carrots was one of the more popular dishes. They traveled quite well, the food tasted good even months later, and despite the obvious flaw of being packed in breakable glass bottles, it was a rousing success.

The guy who invented food preservation may have gotten filthy rich, but who was the real winner? Our fat asses, that's who.

Get a load of *these* cans

The British soon got a hold of this new idea, and they set about improving it for their own navy. They got rid of the silly glass bottles and replaced them with steel cans lined with tin. This new can technique was an amazing leap in human progress. The first canned (or tinned, as the British refer to it) food products became a reality.

For the time being, canned meat products were used only by the military, world explorers, and budding weightlifters. These cans were made of wrought iron lined with a protective layer of tin, so they usually weighed more than the food inside them.

Sadly, the food in these early cans was almost always overcooked. It was better to overcook the meat than risk it going bad. Safety first! This situation would improve after the invention of white lab coats and clipboards.

Despite the availability of quick, convenient foods, many pretentious jackasses still can't get it together.

The world before SPAM

By 1850, drying and salting meat was so totally 1849.

People suffering from the bubonic plague were often treated to a fun-filled visit from the medieval LEECHMOBILE. Huzzah!

One bad can

By the 1850s, the Royal Navy was quite accustomed to purchasing large quantities of tinned meat products, and was naturally trying to get it as cheap as possible. Along comes Mr. Goldner, who had a factory in Moldavia with plenty of cheap labor and even cheaper meat. He sold countless amounts of large (often 12-pound) cans of meat to the British navy. But quite a lot of it was totally putrid when the cans were opened. The cans were simply too large to cook all the way through. This resulted in pockets of bacteria inside the can, which continued to grow as the can sat. Unfortunately, that wasn't the worst of it.

sacré bleu!!

The early cans were made of thick, heavy steel. They were so hard to get into that soldiers were known to shoot them open. Sound stupid? Well, they were also wearing bright colors on the battlefield and got all neatly lined up to slaughter each other.

In 1824 Capt. William Parry sails for the South Pole with tinned meat and balls of steel.

Mr. Goldner had been stuffing the cans with horrible and untasteful things. According to reports, it included "pieces of heart, roots of tongue, pieces of palate, coagulated blood, pieces of liver, ligaments of the throat, pieces of intestine," and who knows what else. Tongues have roots?

Stephen Goldner, you gave canned food a bad name. Throw away our friendship bracelet!!

The Prince of Cans

One person who will always be associated positively with canned goods is Prince Albert. The joy he has brought to prank callers is immeasurable, not to mention the exotic-body-piercing crowd, but he also played an important role in getting the word out on canned foods. With Prince Albert's assistance, London held the Great Exhibition in 1851, where canned foods were all the rage. This was the kind of kickstart that mankind needed to realize the importance of canned food. He also had a magnificent moustache. He will always be in our hearts.

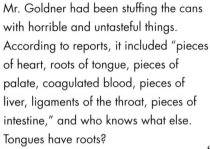

Mary Louise is credited with making the first tin-can telephone. A fun pastime sometimes confused with another game—"shouting at each other really loudly."

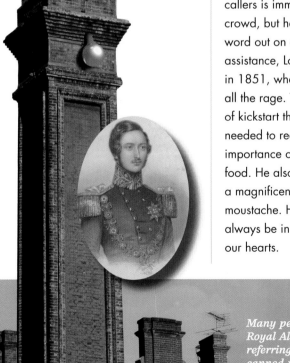

Many people thought this smokestack located next to Royal Albert Hall was the one Prince Albert was referring to when he said, "If you're impressed by my canned pork, you should see my chimney." It's not.

THE HISTORY of CANS

Canning technology is like a woman. There is so much goodness inside.
But how to get that goodness out has always been a challenge.

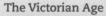

The Victorian Age

These cans were especially difficult.
Much force and prying was required.
Some even resorted to using an ax.

Iron can

Queen Victoria

The Lincolnian Age

While easier to open, these cans still required
the proper tool. Sadly, at the time, it was quite
unladylike to handle tools in such a fashion.

Steel rimmed

Mary Todd Lincoln

The Sexual Revolution

In the interest of being self-sufficient, these cans
came with their own tool. These new cans
could go anywhere. Like into the men's room.

Key

RuPaul

The Victorian Secret Age

This modern version utilizes the same basic structure
of cans, but is ready to go at a moment's notice.
Some say it is so easy, a monkey could do it.

Pop-top

Paris

Slaves out. Cans in.

The small canning factories across the country went into high gear during the Civil War. Union and Confederate soldiers alike were eating canned rations. This turned out to be a great way to get new consumers. It was a brilliant marketing plan, although completely accidental and through highly unfortunate circumstances—what with all the fighting and cannons and scratchy wool uniforms.

When these soldiers went home after the war, they brought with them the promise, convenience, and overall warm, fuzzy feeling of canned goods. By the 1870s, the United States had overtaken the rest of the world in canned goods production. Was canning meat a recipe for becoming the most powerful nation on earth? You be the judge.

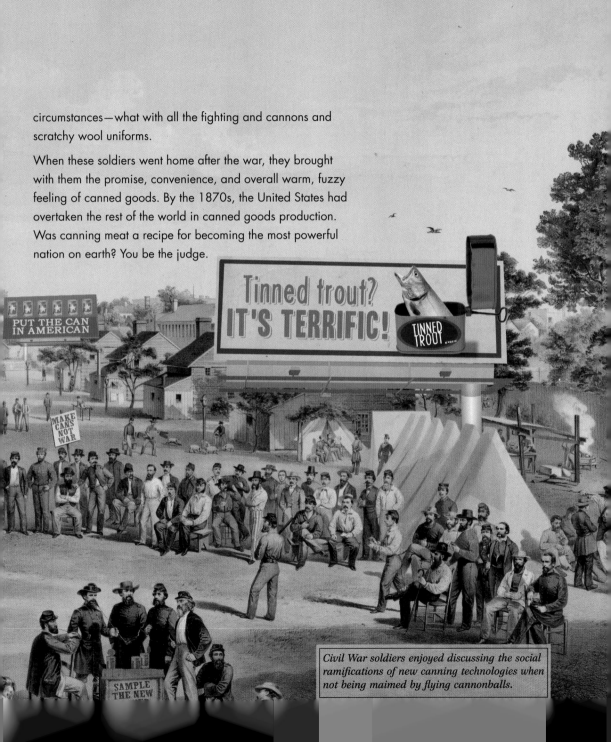

PUT THE CAN IN AMERICAN

Tinned trout? IT'S TERRIFIC!

TINNED TROUT

MAKE CANS NOT WAR

SAMPLE THE NEW

Civil War soldiers enjoyed discussing the social ramifications of new canning technologies when not being maimed by flying cannonballs.

A SPAM IS BORN

The year was 1936. The place was a quiet little town called Austin, Minnesota. The future was about to happen. Did the Earth rumble and the skies part and lightning strike and birds speak and leprechauns dance at the approaching greatness? Could anyone at the time have fathomed how schoolchildren would weep when they heard the amazing story? How the tide of world events would be drastically altered by one simple but perfect idea?

Pork shoulder problems

Jay Hormel had a problem on his hands. In the Hormel plant, some good meat was going to waste. Pork shoulders were not selling like he'd hoped, and much of it had to be thrown out. Pork shoulder is a good, solid, delicious cut of pork. But its shape is not what people were used to. Once removed from the bone, pork shoulder meat is in chunk form. Also, the process of removing it from the bone was rather expensive and time-consuming, especially if it wasn't selling so good. No one was sure what to do with it all.

*Le Boot Camp
à la mode*
Paris

Jay had faced a similar dilemma when he served as an army quartermaster in France during WWI. At the time, tons and tons of beef were being shipped to Europe. The army was shipping the beef with the bone still in. What a silly thing to do. Jay suggested they bone the meat first, and remove all that extra weight and wasted space. Everyone thought this was a grand idea, and he was soon sent back to Chicago, where he showed everybody how to better pack the beef for shipping. The taxpayers were grateful, and the soldiers got more meat. Everybody was a winner. Except the cows.

After work, I get to lick the meat-auger!

HORMEL
Flavor-Sealed
SPICED HAM

By the slice or in 3 or 6 Pound Vacuum Sealed Tins

For $1, you'd get a tour of the plant and a photo with Mildred. She wouldn't hold your hand. But she'd hold your SPAM.

Only 2 million more shovel-loads until retirement!

The ultimate solution

Jay Hormel was never a man to shrink away from a meaty opportunity. The pork shoulder problem at the Hormel plant was about to be turned into one of the greatest products of all time.

Hormel had already become canning geniuses over the years. But now they started to experiment on a super-sexy pork shoulder and ham canned combo. It was hard work to find just the right recipe. The flavor, texture, purity, and look all were painstakingly analyzed. Heck, they're still adjusting the formula now and again. Eventually, the right combination was achieved and it was ready to go to market. All they needed was a way to tell the world about it.

They didn't really need to record how many pigs were killed each day. It just helped when they had to let the hogs know who's boss.

Margie here made the billionth can of SPAM. That meant a $5 bonus and an upgrade for her dental plan.

This apron protects my pants. And my dignity.

Painting is delicate work.
Just like carving up a pig!

A SPAM IS BORN

What's in a name?

What's a snazzy product without a snazzy name? In order to get the attention of American housewives in the late 30s, you had to hit them with razzmatazz and jazzy jingles. Jay put out an APB that he'd give $100 in cold, hard cash to anyone who could come up with a name for his canned pork shoulder product. After several hundred were collected, they had "Brunch" and "Baby Grand." What kind of knuckleheads were these people?

The New Year's Eve party

The clock was ticking. Jay was getting nervous. So he threw a New Year's Eve bash with a special rule. If you wanted a free drink, you had to write down a name idea. The little slips of paper piled up quickly. Jay was later quoted as saying, "Along about the fourth or fifth drink they began showing some imagination." Still, it was mostly crap. Good thing Kenneth Daigneau found his way to the party.

DJ Palooka swung the phat beats old school. It was positively ducky!

Over the years, many have tried to lay claim to coming up with the name. Some have even tried to cover up the New Year's Eve party, but Jay himself owned up to it years later. Things sure get persnickety when there's a Franklin involved.

He who nameth SPAM

Kenneth Daigneau was an actor from New York and was probably quite dapper. Legend has it that he blurted out the word "SPAM" at some point during Jay's party. The Earth must have stopped moving for just a moment as everyone's eyes turned to his, knowing in their hearts that their lives would never be the same. Or maybe nobody heard it but Jay. Nevertheless, Jay loved the name SPAM and Kenneth was $100 richer.

Why SPAM?

Many have speculated that he formed the word based on the attributes of the product, "spiced ham" or "shoulder of pork and ham." Yeah, maybe. That sounds good. Let's go with that.

Kenny's payday

What could Kenneth Daigneau have purchased with $100 in 1937? Candy was a penny and sodas were a nickel. And a trip to the dentist's cost you a fiver. But in today's money, it would be roughly $1,300. That's at least two pieces of really nice bling or some totally sweet ground effects for a Ford Escort station wagon.

THE MEAT THAT WON THE WAR

Many people think that World War II was the reason SPAM was created. Wrong! SPAM was already being ravenously consumed nationwide. It just so happens that it was also the perfect fit for military service and humanitarian aid. We all should be thankful that SPAM was so versatile. Some even go so far as to say that without SPAM, the Allies could not have won the war. It was a proud time to be meat.

This ain't our war

When Hitler's tanks rolled across Europe in 1939, the prevailing opinion in the United States was to stay out of the conflict. The thought of entering the war and coming to the aid of our allies in Great Britain, France, and elsewhere was hotly debated all over the country.

Jay Hormel, a veteran of WWI, felt so strongly against the war at the time that he commissioned a song.

The lyrics went something like this:

Not unless they come a-knockin' at our door!
If they want to fight each other, well it's none of our affair;
We haven't any mothers with an extra son to spare;
Let's sing "God Bless America" instead of "Over There."
THIS AIN'T OUR WAR!

While there is no historical record of the choreography intended to accompany this ditty, the reader should keep in mind that "jazz hands" were not invented yet.

Help is on the way

In March 1941, the United States decided to help our European allies with support "just short of war." This meant tanks and jeeps and gasoline and guns and ammunition and clothes and countless other things, including plenty of SPAM. It was called the Lend-Lease program. By October 1941, President Roosevelt approved lending over $1 billion in aid to Great Britain alone. It's taken quite a while to pay back.

Guilt trips like these ensured that decapitated soldiers still got plenty to eat.

Soon, the Hormel plant was churning out all kinds of goods for the Lend-Lease program. SPAM, among many other Hormel products, was being shipped overseas to help out Allied forces and civilians from many countries.

When SPAM first hit the UK, they didn't quite understand the name. Many guessed it stood for Supply Processed American Meat, Specially Processed Army Meat, and possibly even So Pretty And Munchycrunchers. Fine. Maybe not that last one, but at least they never doubted it was meat.

Margaret Thatcher ate a lot of SPAM. She later became Prime Minister. Coincidence?

One of the first "embedded journalists," Edward R. Murrow won many awards for reporting about SPAM and other war stuff. He should have got an award for awesome neckwear.

SLAMMIN' SPAMMY

Once you awaken the pink dragon, there's no stopping it. Prepare to be attacked with bombs of deliciousness and nutrition.

Pearl Harbor: it's go time

On the fateful day of December 7th, 1941, the Japanese were obviously looking for a beating. The United States immediately declared war on the Axis powers, and the entire country went on full alert. It was totally on.

This meant much tighter security at the Hormel plant, which was of vital importance to the war effort. Military intelligence was way better back then. Successfully sabotaging the Hormel plant could mean countless people around the world would go hungry. So they put huge lights on the new steel fence surrounding the plant and guarded it 24-7. So don't even try it, Adolf! You're not getting into this plant. You either, Yamamoto!

Every employee was issued an official Hormel identification badge. If you forgot your badge, you didn't get in. Rules is rules. You had to have a badge. Seriously. You needed a badge to get in. That's why they made them. Don't try to fake one with a Bedazzler. Cuz it ain't gonna work.

Routine inspections of the plant by military personnel became, well . . . routine. Fresh meat was a huge priority for the inspectors. It had the most potential for going bad before it got to the foxholes. SPAM was poked and prodded and had comments written about it on clipboards. Sadly, the reports were often illegible due to the smeared gel.

"There were many jokes going around in the army, some of them off-color, about American SPAM; it tasted good nonetheless. Without SPAM, we wouldn't have been able to feed our army."
—Soviet premier Nikita Khrushchev, quoted in Khrushchev Remembers

If you forgot your badge, your kids just wouldn't eat that week. Them's the breaks.

By 1944, a full 90 percent of Hormel's canned food output was going directly to the Armed Forces. The war years proved to be Hormel's busiest. Just between 1939 and 1942, Hormel's sales doubled and annual pork processing hit an all-time high of 1.6 million head. That's a whole lot of hogs. By April of 1945, over 100 million pounds of SPAM had fed hungry soldiers and civilians overseas. That's the equivalent of over 133 million cans of SPAM.

Each can was doubly inspected for sabotage. These ladies made sure no Nazis were hiding inside the SPAM.

Where was SPAMVILLE? Wedged right between Shirtlessville and Moustache City.

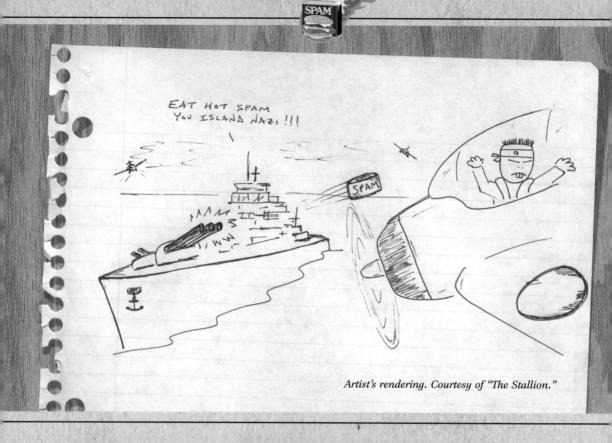

Artist's rendering. Courtesy of "The Stallion."

SPAM:1 Zero:0

THE AMAZING AND POSSIBLY TRUE STORY OF HOW
ONE MAN TURNED SPAM INTO SPAMMUNITION

On a navy ship in the South Pacific, one of the cooks aboard would take a can of SPAM for himself when supplies ran low. This was a big no-no, so he'd hide the can by tying a string around it and throwing it down the barrel of one of the big guns.

One day, there was a kamikaze attack. There was no time for the cook to grab his beloved can of SPAM. All the rounds fired from the ship missed the kamikaze. But somehow the Japanese Zero crashed into the sea anyway. According to legend, the hidden can of SPAM was shot out of the barrel and flew through the glass canopy of the attacking plane, killing the Japanese pilot. SPAM saved the day. Now, while the truth of this story may come under question, this is not the only time SPAM has been used as a weapon. While surely not the intent of Mr. Jay Hormel, it certainly speaks to the incredible versatility of the product.

"WHAT'RE WE HAVING FOR CHOW TONIGHT?"
—Sgt. Tom Zibelli

"IF WORST COMES TO WORST, WE CAN ALWAYS EAT THE SPAM."
—Pfc. Joe Kramer

"I'VE GOT IT! SOMETHING REALLY DIFFERENT! WE'LL SLICE THE SPAM LENGTHWISE!"
—Pvt. Thomas F. Flannery

Pfc. Frank A. Hewitt in Our Army

"Next time you stuff the turkey with Spam open the can!"

Because of its portability and stay-goodness, canned luncheon meat ended up being served to American soldiers two or even three times a day. No wonder the GIs were so frustrated. They often referred to SPAM as the "meat that failed its physical."

I STILL DON'T WANT ANY SPAM!!

YANK

THE SAD SACK   "SPAM"

A Sad Sack of Mail

Not all SPAM was SPAM

You heard it. Some SPAM served during WWII was not SPAM at all. SPAM became the moniker for any canned luncheon meat served over there. Many pork-processing plants across the country were contributing to the war effort. Were those other meat products made up to the high standards of SPAM? Obviously not.

"Whadya mean luncheon meat?
I say it's Spam and I say to hell with it!"

Goodness me! Racy cartoons like these sure seem out of place today. You'd never see Garfield swearing at someone. He does such funny stuff. Like wear sunglasses. LOL!

THEY'RE SERVING SPAM TONIGHT
(From an Army newspaper)

In the days before "don't ask, don't tell," many French maidens were left confused.

A 12-ounce can of SPAM is plenty to feed a small family. But a whole battalion of beefy uniformed men? The army requested their meat come in bigger sizes, specifically 6-pound cans. That's eight times bigger than a can of SPAM. To make matters worse, the army demanded it be cooked longer. This certainly removes any risk from bacteria, but it also ruins the flavor and texture of the meat. With that in mind, it is no wonder that SPAM started getting such a bad name among GIs.

Can I get SPAM today?

ABSOLUTELY! Uncle Sam has okayed the use of tin for Spam ... enough now to make it available to you as well as the armed forces and our allies. Your grocer's stocks have been replenished. Right now, you can count on Spam for wartime meal-planning!

And that's great news, because it's so easy to prepare nourishing, vitamin-rich meals with Spam.

Spam 'n Spaghetti, Spam 'n Beans, Spamwiches made with enriched bread. Spam fits in naturally with almost every one of the delicious, nutritious foods your government wants you to serve.

Ask your grocer for Spam today ... and for a real treat, try one of Spam's delightful Victory Meals pictured below. Geo. A. Hormel & Co., Austin, Minnesota.

SPAM 'N BEANS: Place thin Spam slices atop casserole of canned baked beans—sprinkle with brown sugar—bake until bubbly. Plenty of solid nourishment. Quick and inexpensive!

SPAM 'N SPAGHETTI: Quickly brown several thick Spam slices in hot frying pan. Serve with spaghetti or macaroni and cheese casserole topped with buttered bread crumbs. Delicious!

Many people were angered by stateside SPAM shortages during the war. Meanwhile countless GIs wanted to send it back. Ahhh. The irony.

THE ULTIMATE BOMB SHELTER

YOUR HOME-AWAY-FROM-HELL-ON-EARTH

This door must be really thick. To keep the mutants out and your freshness in.

The apocalypse may make people crazy. Automatic weapons keep them sane. Or else.

It may take years before the surface is radiation-free. Best to get only one kind of food. Variety is for apocalyptic zombies.

Fondue pots brighten up any party. Anyone who survived Armageddon will enjoy the burning-hot oil!

Yesterday's fear is today's humor!

Remember when Armageddon was just around the corner? What a chuckle. Now that we're Armageddon-free, bomb shelters like these need to find a new purpose. Now they can be used for S&M dungeons, underground marijuana fields, or animal-testing labs.

Serving SPAM to a returning GI was not such a good idea. You can always have too much of a good thing. Unless we're talking about kisses from a kitten.

Welcome home, have a sandwich

Despite all the hard feelings from GIs during the war, tempers died down after victory was achieved and the true sentiment started to come out again. Need proof? Get ready for this: General Eisenhower himself sent a letter to Hormel President H. H. Corey. It's a shout-out to his Austin homeys and a heartfelt confession from the most powerful man in the free world.

When the GIs returned home, SPAM sales continued to climb. It seems that despite the grumblings and misunderstandings, quite a lot of veterans still had a special place in their hearts for SPAM.

The shirtless foam parties on Iwo Jima made breakfast really awkward.

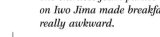

HEY, LOOK!

A LETTER FROM PRESIDENT EISENHOWER TO THE PRESIDENT OF HORMEL!

Who's awesome now?

DDE

GETTYSBURG
PENNSYLVANIA 17325

June 29, 1966

My dear Tim:

I have just learned from our mutual friend, Jack Cornelius, that your company is celebrating its seventy-fifth anniversary in business.

May I offer you my heartiest congratulations.

You might be surprised to learn that I have long felt a certain kinship with your company.

During World War II, of course, I ate my share of SPAM along with millions of other soldiers. I'll even confess to a few unkind remarks about it -- uttered during the strain of battle, you understand. But as former Commander in Chief, I believe I can still officially forgive you your only sin: sending us so much of it.

Later, as a somewhat inexperienced political candidate, I shared with you the friendship and wise counsel of your advertising agency, BBDO. I must say, I believe they had a tougher job with me than selling SPAM to ex-servicemen. Happily, we all succeeded together.

One more thing we have in common -- our enthusiasm for golf. Were it possible, I would enjoy a round with you very much. But, Tim, I'm afraid you'd have to slow down your whirlwind pace a bit. I have this old "football knee" that nags me, but as a player yourself, I know you understand.

My very best wishes to you and to your company for its continuing success.

Sincerely yours

Dwight D. Eisenhower

Mr. H. H. Corey
Hormel Company
Austin, Minnesota

Just because he was an 83-star general doesn't mean he didn't eat his share of SPAM. He also went on to become U.S. President. Mmmmm. Powerful.

SPAM COOKING 101
FROSTED COOKIES

1. OK, so like I'm out here all alone in the woods And being alone always makes me hungry.

2. So good thing I brought some SPAM, right? I'm totally going to make SPAM frosted cookies.

3. I love cooking SPAM when I'm all by myself. It looks so hot, all fried up and everything.

4. Then I frost them with mashed potatoes.
   Oh wait, I got some on my finger.
   Let me slowly lick it off.

5. OMG! What is that creepy bear doing here?
   He's totally invading my personal space!

6. Not the teeth! I just got my braces off!

7. (quiet bleeding)

SPAM
FAMILY
TREE

It takes all kinds of SPAM to make the world go 'round. That's why SPAM comes in many different forms. It could be because SPAM has mystical self-changing powers. It could also be that through carefully thought out line extensions, SPAM has reached even more people than you could count on a hundred million fingers.

This is only a small representation of every SPAM label design.
To show them all would require billions of pages and lay waste to our forests.

There are only 7 colors in the rainbow. But look at all these
different kinds of SPAM. It makes rainbows look like total idiots.

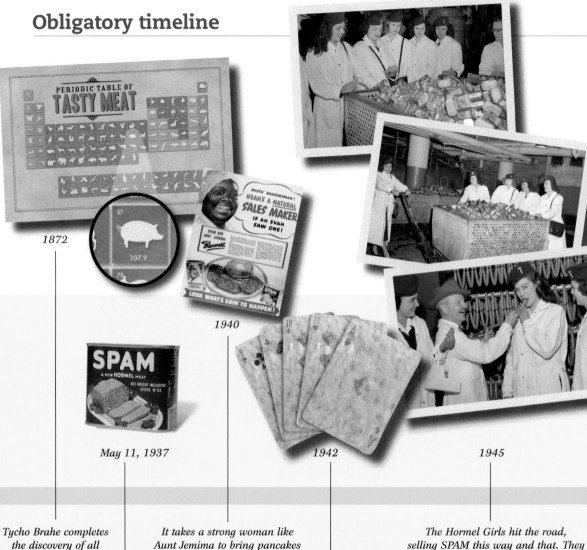

1872

1940

May 11, 1937

1942

1945

Tycho Brahe completes the discovery of all things meaty. There was no organism he did not taste.

It takes a strong woman like Aunt Jemima to bring pancakes and SPAM together.

The Hormel Girls hit the road, selling SPAM this way and that. They later had a hit CBS Radio show every Saturday night to showcase their talents. Also, they loved hot dogs.

SPAM is invented. This puts canned meat on the map. Permanent freshness is here to stay.

Innovative American soldiers find yet another use for SPAM. Table maximum was two coconuts.

"It's a **SPAM**-dandy"

1997

$2

Scratch the play area. Match the number of "SPAM" symbols to the prize grid to determine prize won. Get a " " symbol in any spot, win $5. Get a " " symbol in any spot, win $100. Get a " " symbol in any spot, win $500.

Minnesota State Lottery

Over 170,000 prizes of $10 and higher!

Win up to $25,000!

PRIZE GRID

10	SPAM	$25,000
9	SPAM	$2,500
8	SPAM	$1,000
7	SPAM	$400
6	SPAM	$200
5	SPAM	$40
4	SPAM	$20
3	SPAM	$10
2	SPAM	$3
1	SPAM	$2

VOID

1980s

1987

1996

2000

The 50th birthday of SPAM calls for the biggest party in the world, complete with a boombox blasting out Whitesnake and Wang Chung.

SPAM finally takes its rightful spot in the Smithsonian National Museum of American History. Probably next to Fonzie's jacket. Special watermelon blazers were used for the occasion.

Illiteracy was such a rampant problem in the 80s, even advertising executives couldn't read. Thankfully America was saved by Hooked on Phonics.

The SPAMBURGER Hamburger craze consumes America. It completes the redundancy trend started by Duran Duran, Sirhan Sirhan, and Boutros Boutros-Ghali.

SPAM gets into the gambling racket with a scratch-off lottery ticket. Now SPAM can bring you even more happiness. And maybe some money.

2013

2004

2005

2007

Monty Python's SPAMALOT becomes the darling of Broadway. SPAM celebrates all the singing and violence with a new flavor, SPAM Golden Honey Grail. Turns out elderberries were disgusting.

Expanding into the frozen treat market, SPAMSICLES are a wild success. Sucking on meat has never been more refreshing!

SPAM Singles are developed. Finally, SPAM can be enjoyed alone, in peace. Without all the nagging and the "when are you going to paint the garage?"

The publishing world is redefined as the most informative book ever written is revealed to the American public. The Internet and daytime cable television are totally forgotten for 12 minutes.

2052

2086

2162

Science finally proves the existence of a SPAM side effect that drastically improves personality. It is universally prescribed to all in this convenient pill form.

When the metal ones come, humanity will flee from planet to planet. Luckily, satellite-transmissible SPAM will be beamed directly into your helmet.

As life becomes more and more hectic, using one's mouth to eat will be a luxury for the super-ultra-rich. The development of direct-injection SPAM made from hydroponic pork becomes as popular as spray-on socks.

"It was then she realized she'd never been this hungry before. She needed the pink meat at all costs. Grasping the can firmly, she pulled the ring. With abandon, she rapidly shook the can until slowly the meat showed itself with a light glisten. Now she would taste it. But she still played coy, not wanting to let on how many times she had tasted it before."

—excerpt from "The Ecstasy of Wilbur" by Alexa Steele

Do you not respect?
I eat the SPAM for power
Strength through SPAM loving.

Don't just **make friends,** make your friends SPAM sandwiches.

ZORG7192's SPAM Haiku

SPAM MART

"Where quality meets tasty"

The real reason America was invented!

SPAM™ Do-It-Yourself Tattoo Kit — $19.77
Prison quality, right in your home!

SPAM™ Cookies — $1.95
Tastes great going down OR coming up!

SPAM™ Shampoo — $6.99
Give your hair that SPAM shine.

SPAM™ Workout Video — $10.26
Feel the burn of this 12-oz. routine.

Frosted SPAM™ Cereal — $3.95
Stays meaty even in milk!

SPAM® 'n' Cookie Sandwiches — $2.95 FOR 4!
Salty and sweet sure is neat!

SPAM™ Ice Cream — $4.99
Even pigs scream for this ice cream.

NEW!

Spray-On SPAM™ — $7.95
Finally get SPAM into those hard-to-reach places!

SPAM™ Energy Drink — $1.25
For your on-the-go pork lifestyle.

SPAM™ Soda Pop — $1.99 6-PACK!
The bubbles mean it's working!

The savings will blow your mind, the flavor will blow your mouth.

$2.95

SPAM™ Mouthwash

Fights gingivitis with the power of protein!

$4.95

SPAM™ Pain-B-Gone!

Not intended for recreational use.

$1.99

SPAM™ Gum

Now with longer-lasting meat flavor!

$7.95

SPAM™ Eyedrops

Hide your late-night SPAM™ benders from your boss!

Convenient choices, satisfying values

$7.95

SPAM™ MEGA Clean

Experience the cleansing power of pork.

$29.99

SPAM™ Perfume

Most perfumes are made from pig pheromones anyway. NOT A JOKE

$2.95

SPAM™ Hand Soap

Nothing works better on stripper glitter.

IMPROVED FORMULA!

$1.95

SPAM™ Toothpaste

Have that SPAM-fresh feeling all day long!

Bring all your money!

99¢

SPAM™ Dental Floss

Fill your tooth crevices with something meaty.

$3.95

SPAM™ Baby Lotion

Cover up that icky baby smell with sweet-ass meat.

$2.89

SPAM™ Deodorant

The fastest way to be raped by a moose.

2 for $10

SPAM™-Flavored Booze

Packed with protein for a raging buzz.

BUT ONCE THEY REALIZE WE HAVE EMBRACED SPAM AS THE ULTIMATE ANSWER TO THE UNIVERSE, THEY DECIDE WE MUST BE WORSHIPPED AS GODS THROUGH AN AGGRESSIVE INTER-STELLAR CAMPAIGN OF BEAR HUGS & SLOPPY KISSES, DRUNKEN PHONE CALLS, AND RANDOM PROBINGS.

BEYOND THE MOUTH
Taking SPAM from can to canvas

"TASTY RAINBOW"

Andy Warhol supposedly tinkered with SPAM cans before deciding to go with Campbell's soup cans instead. He liked the vertical nature better. Sounds perverted to us.

"FUTURE SPAM"

In this horrific view of the future, giant mutant children befriend pigs only to force them to live in giant SPAM cans. In the hearts of children there is evil.

"ERE THE SLAUGHTER"

Some artists are inspired to paint still lifes, sweeping landscapes, or intimate portraits, or to comment on social issues. Others want to carve meandering pigs out of wood.

"PILLOW DANCER"

This is Pillow. She's a dancer. She's a SPAM fan. She's a visitor from a faraway land. Where headgear is more important than modesty, there is no shame, and SPAM is king.

The saga begins! SPAM has a new name and a whole new look. Yellow and blue were popular back then, as was knowing the weight of juices.

LABELS
A GAME ABOUT MOVING FORWARD

It's not really a game. It was the only interesting way to present the history of the SPAM labels.

START

1936

1937

1938

1943

Before SPAM was SPAM, there was this stuff. It so obviously needed to change.

Darn Nazis! Little did they know how they'd affect everything, even the colors used to paint a SPAM can.

SPAM is no longer new, so that line had to go. But it did gain "the meat of many uses." That was also my nickname in high school.

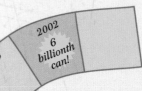

Turns out no one bakes a SPAM loaf anymore. Did they ever? This 2-month special edition can gives us a hint of the future.

2002
6 billionth can!

1996

1994
5 billionth can!

1992

After five years of denial, it is finally determined that, in fact, no one bakes SPAM. It's much better in a burger. They call it an epiphany. We call it 20 years too late.

1987

1986
4 billionth can!

The advent of porkupuncture led to many new piercing SPAM dishes. The logo was getting a little fat. Time to hit the gym, typeface!

1980
3 billionth can!

1970
2 billionth can!

1959
1 billionth can!

1950s

Catching up with the times, SPAM's new 1987 logo looks like it came right out of the 70s! Notice the photorealistic loaf.

MONTY PYTHON'S
SPAMALOT

A new musical *lovingly* ripped off from the motion picture
MONTY PYTHON and the Holy Grail

For decades, Broadway has been the land of overdone dance numbers and retardulous song lyrics. Now this level of silliness has been raised to new heights. Except this time, it's meant to be funny. SPAMALOT is the Pythons' first foray into musicals, and it won them the Tony for Best Musical in 2005. Now it will probably tour the country forever and ever.

— drunken artist's rendering

SPAMALOT THE MUSICAL

page 72

ALL KNIGHTS:

SPAM

Please enjoy this SPAM-related excerpt from the script for SPAMALOT. For your own protection, the rest of the script has been hidden from your view.

SPAM®

When you say the word "SPAM," most people assume you're talking about junk emails. Unfortunately, spam (notice the use of lowercase) is everywhere and EVERYONE hates it. Junk emails are boring and reprehensible and just plain scandalous.

Why did they come to be called spam emails? There are many theories. Most of which include the Monty Python SPAM skit. In said skit, Vikings sing the famous SPAM song, filling the air with SPAM and flooding our ears with joy. Since this is much like how your inbox can be swamped with junk mail, the connection was made to call it spam. Supposedly.

spam

Another story makes its origin seem not so clever. Back in the day when the Internet didn't have pictures, everybody had to just type at each other. That was boring. So instead, they annoyed each other by repeating the Monty Python SPAM SPAM SPAM song in their messages. This made everyone's eyes bleed from reading it thousands of times. Those restless over-typers were called "spammers." The first time it became associated with schlocky advertising was in 1994 when a law firm specializing in green card and other immigration cases started posting their text ads on all kinds of discussion groups. Since then it has gotten out of control. It's the first sign of the apocalypse.

READING THE FUNNY NUMBERS OR "HOW ROBOTS ARE

RS
BEST BY
EST 199
A

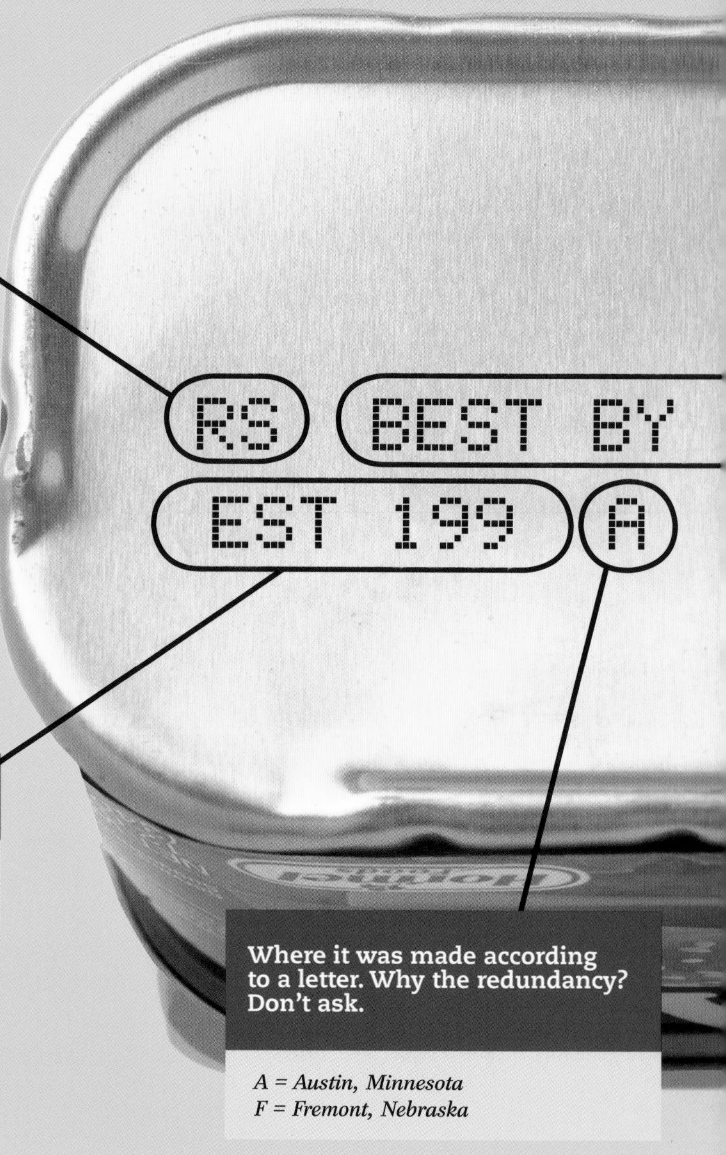

What SPAM variety you're holding

RS = Regular Classic SPAM
TS = Oven-Roasted Turkey
LS = Lite
SM = Smoke-Flavored
DLSS = 25% Less Sodium
TABS = Hot & Spicy
BCN = With Bacon
CHS = With Cheese
HNY = Honey Golden Grail
BBQ = Barbecue Flavor

Where it was made according to its fancy USDA plant code

199 = Austin, Minnesota
199N = Fremont, Nebraska

Where it was made according to a letter. Why the redundancy? Don't ask.

A = Austin, Minnesota
F = Fremont, Nebraska

"Best by" date

This is the last possible month you can enjoy the magical flavors of SPAM before that flavor might be not as magical. "But I thought you said SPAM's cooking process made it permanently fresh." True, but all good things must come to an end. Why are we arguing, anyway? It's not like something this delicious would have the chance of lasting that long. Pop that top already!

What time this slice of heaven was born, using military time

For those not familiar with military time, just subtract 12 from the hour if it's over 12. So this can was made at 1:58 p.m. How fun was that to figure out? Now drop and give me 20.

DEC 2012

11294 2 13:58

Canning time period

This SPAM was canned in period 2. No human knows what that means. Let's just hope lunch is period 3. Fingers crossed!!!

This can's birthday. Cake and pony rides for everyone!

11/29/4 or November 29th, 2004

SPAM ADVERTISING

How did you find out about SPAM? Were you born with the knowledge of the Great Perfection? Did your mother tell you? Did you learn about it in school? Did you learn it on the streets from those kids you weren't supposed to be hanging around with? Chances are, you've seen a SPAM advertisement that implanted the Sublime Knowledge into your noodle. Let's relive those magical moments together.

"Look! There's my pet pig, Trixie! She looks delicious!"

Sell! Sell! Sell!

It may be astounding, but there was a time when SPAM was so new to the world that no one knew what it was. Industry analysts at the time reported that SPAM wouldn't sell to American housewives. They didn't understand what to do with it. Jay Hormel looked at the findings and scoffed, "Nuts. It just hasn't been sold right—let's get started."

Using the brave headline "Hormel Announces SPAM," these color newspaper ads quickly told everybody what the real deal was. Eating SPAM was awesome, and everyone knew it—after they saw these ads. One of the ads was put on the back cover of TIME magazine, and quickly thereafter, national demand for the "miracle meat" went through the roof.

SPAM, SPAM, SPAM, SPAM
Hormel's new miracle meat in a can
Saves time, tastes fine
To eat something grand, ask for SPAM!

This first radio jingle for SPAM is also argued to be the first radio jingle ever! Can you hear it? No. Because books are stupid and don't play MP3s.

Could these ads be produced today? No way. Not in this politically correct day and age. Family-style tickling is not allowed. Way too provocative.

While it is hard to discern what the slang meanings of "trick" and "picnic" may have been at the time of this ad, we certainly can see that her customers are quite satisfied with her offerings.

Maybe his cap is on too tight, because how hard is it to figure out what a SPAM bake is? Jeepers creepers, that guy must be dumb.

This guy has it going on. He's rapping way before rapping was invented, his girl don't talk too much, and he's grilling SPAM. His SPAMBURGER is minimalistic and pure. He is legend.

Fun to read, and fun to remember days gone by when men were given the respect they so dearly deserved. Model citizens, one and all. Yes, dear, you may wash the car now.

George and Gracie

Sure, it was a wildly successful product launch. But that wasn't enough for Jay Hormel. He wanted SPAM to get noticed. So he took it right to the top.

George Burns and his wife, Gracie Allen, had the hottest show on the radio. Almost every American across the country listened to *The Burns and Allen Show* on NBC. It was the perfect way to tell millions of people about the majesty of SPAM. They even had a pet pig named SPAMMY. Totally cute. Totally delicious.

Make your own vintage ad!

1. Choose an awkward visual

2. Match it to an uncomfortable caption!

"Boy, I'm beat!"
"Then you need meat!"

"Gee, lunch looks so pretty."
"I have no other marketable skills."

"Your hat looks really stupid."
"It's so those dirty Commies can't listen to my thoughts."

"Where'd you learn to cook? Clown school?"
"I want a divorce."

"Is SPAM for real, G?"
"Holla holla, yo!"

"Will you ever think of me in prison?"
"Only at lunchtime!"

"I'm glad we joined the hat gang."
"Hats are mad fresh!"

"Life is grand, ain't it?"
"Please just let me call my family."

"Why are we playing cards?"
"I'll smack you in the mouth if you sass me again."

"All I can hear is a dial tone."
"That's cuz SPAM is off da hook!"

LEARNING IS IMPORTANT. Here's what we can learn from early SPAM ads:

Magicians think women are stupid.

SPAM will land you a man, even if that's all you got going on.

Using gelled meat to get your closeted husband to spend time with you is the oldest trick in the book. Shame on you.

Ladies talking to each other about what makes their "points go 'round" sells meat. Look into it.

If your kids want to play "soldier," let them. It's an easy way to trick them into forced labor.

Men admiring each other's "lunch boxes" is no substitute for real substance. It's what's inside that counts.

Children need role models. That's what advertising is for.

Psychic abilities among welders is far more common than people would think.

Find these items:

- ☐ moustaches (2)
- ☐ a depressed man who won't get out of bed
- ☐ 12 fried eggs
- ☐ a telegram
- ☐ a soldier
- ☐ canned hams (2)
- ☐ female coworkers asking very personal questions
- ☐ the poor wife of grumpy-ass Keith Holton
- ☐ some bitchin' saddle shoes
- ☐ dangerously sharp knives (4)

Good luck!

This painting captures the loneliness and solitude of the meat inside the can. The reflection here denotes the confidence and hope of SPAM. The juxtaposition of the two evokes an acknowledgment of a sensory explosion, hinting at the true meaning of SPAM.

*The future of recycling is
here, and man is it sexy.*

Recipes that time forgot. For a reason.

Ah' inspiring...
SPAM 'N' LIMAS

SPAM 'N' LIMAS
FROM THE HORMEL MENU FILES

COLD OR HOT
SPAM HITS THE SPOT!

HORMEL
GOOD FOODS

Right on the beam...
PLANKED SPAM

PLANKED SPAM

SPAM HITS THE SPOT!

HORMEL
GOOD FOODS

Does SPAM taste great? Of course. Does it taste even better when you pair it with the blandest food on Earth? Great guns, yes! Can't you just hear the marketing team unravel? It is a beautiful shot, to be sure. Maybe it even tastes OK. But they have to be grabbing at straws at this point.

Avast, mateys! This is the first evidence of a pirate theme in the world of SPAM. Instead of walking the plank, you're cooking SPAM on it! Sadly, this also may be the last pirate reference.

Festive! Fun to make!
SPAM UPSIDE DOWN PIE

SPAM UPSIDE DOWN PIE

A supper that sings!
SPAM BIRDS

SPAM BIRDS

HORMEL
GOOD FOODS

COLD OR HOT...
SPAM HITS THE SPOT!

Square Meal!
SPAM 'N' YAMS

SPAM 'N' YAMS

COLD OR HOT SPAM HITS THE SPOT!

HORMEL
GOOD FOODS

If you thought SPAM was awesome normal-ways, try flipping it upside down! Works in the kitchen, works in the bedroom. We read that in Cosmo.

Tweet tweet! What was that, pretty birdy made of pig? Don't fly away. That wouldn't be delicious at all. That's why we stuck toothpicks in your wings. Who's tweeting now?

Does the little porcelain puppy want some SPAM? Does it look good to you, tiny alabaster buddy? NO! You must hold the bulbous plant! Forever!

Happy Blending
BAKED BEAN SPAM'WICH

BAKED BEAN SPAM'WICH

Sunday night delight
SPAM 'N' CUSTARD

SPAM 'N' CUSTARD

It's a good feeling to know you're eating a wonderful baked bean sandwich. It's an even better feeling to know that your meal is being watched over by Satan. Or at least his representative salt and pepper shakers.

Is this some kind of a meat dessert? Custard and olives seems to be a wonderful pairing, too. Did they taste any of these before they took the pictures? Betcha somebody lost their job after this one.

Summer-Night Sensation
SPAM 'N' CHEESE RIBBON LOAF

SPAM 'N' CHEESE RIBBON LOAF

COLD OR HOT SPAM HITS THE SPOT

HAPPY PLATE MATES...
SPAM DUTCH OVEN DINNER

SPAM DUTCH OVEN DINNER

SPAM 'N' MACARONI LOAF

COLD OR HOT
SPAM HITS THE SPOT!

California Fiesta

SPAM 'N' YAM FIESTA LOAF
...luscious with cling peaches from California

Summer sunshine for a winter meal! Simply cut a SPAM loaf in two crosswise. Between the two layers, spread canned sweet potatoes, mashed and seasoned. Surround with golden cling peaches from California. Top with "fan" of peach slices. Drizzle on peach juice seasoned with ⅓ teaspoon prepared mustard. Bake in moderately hot oven (400°) 30 to 35 minutes. Extra-good eating because there's ham in SPAM. Try this famous Hormel blend of sweet juicy pork shoulder with mild tender ham.

COLD OR HOT SPAM HITS THE SPOT!

Is SPAM between the cheese, or is cheese betwixt the SPAM? Either way, the best things in life are layered and served with deviled eggs. That's one to grow on.

Isn't a "Dutch oven" a gassy trick you pull on your lady before she wakes up? Now you know it's also something even more deliciously sinful! Let's hope those aren't eyeballs they're serving it with.

Fiestas are Mexican. California is not. How do you bring the two together? Yams. Lots of yams surrounded by peaches. It makes you forget all about the smog and your illegal-alien status.

FIND THE CAN OF SPAM.

You probably think the SPAM is in a taxi. Well, you're wrong. The taxi is just a metaphor for your heart. A little SPAM is inside each and every one of us. Don't believe me? Rip open your chest and prove us wrong.

Even sandwiches fantasize about threesomes.

Happiest meat? I'll show you some happy meat.

But you may not like the gas factory you'll become if you eat all those beans and onions.

The warm, fuzzy feeling you are experiencing has been scientifically predicted. With the images successfully stored in your mind, one taste of SPAM will complete the brainstate and another SPAM fan will be created. This is not evil. It is for your own good.

Oh, I get it. Lots of different "sandwiches." Only one "meat." Naughty.

Look! The SPAM is trying to escape out the sides!

This is what your skull would look like after an eagle attack.

Girls wearing SPAM shirts get all the action, no matter how high-waisted their jeans are. Notice the visual metaphor of white shirts as slices of white bread. Also, their adventurous nature is forgiven by the fact that they are obviously students. Or at least the one on the left is. Get learning!

Let us learn about our-
selves by traveling back
to 1985 suburbia with
the contemporary family
and their nonoffensive
lifestyle that coincides
with sharply defined
demographic profiles.

*Busy basketball daughter rushes up
the stairs, brushing past Dad, who
deftly moves the full laundry basket
he is carrying out of her way.*

*Dad looks back and wonders why
his daughter no longer loves him.
Is it because he only cares about
folding clothes?*

*The idea is revealed to be SPAM.
The Great Perfection was sent from
Hormel through the phone lines.*

*The sparkles are not a video parlor
trick. No, this was a new can-open-
ing technique from Hormel and
renowned magician Doug Henning.*

*The Magic Sparkle-tron not only
opens the can, it also makes a
SPAM dish for you. It turned out to
be too costly to bring to market.*

*Unaware as little Judy approaches,
Dad is in for a surprise. She has
killed before and will kill again.*

*Only through careful negotiation
will Dad survive. His life depends
on it!*

*Now he remembers what will satiate
this beast he created! There is only
one answer.*

*With Judy powerless, the family can
eat together again. This time with
SPAM pizza! SPAM PIZZA PARTY!*

*"Son, this SPAM is so good, I for-
give you for failing history class."*

*"Really? Awesome! Because I failed
geometry, too!"*

Mom is on the phone. With who? Maybe it's whoever taught her to tie that awful thing around her neck?

Basketball girl is hungry. A lifestyle of heavy physical activity has left her volatile and the family walks on eggshells around her.

Something has happened to Mom. The corded telephone and recent near-death experience have helped trigger an enormous idea.

Due to self-esteem issues, Mom is working out her torso area.

It is no coincidence that her workout is so aggressive that it blocks Dad from moving through the den.

Finally, the source of all her body-image woes gets past her exaggerated exercise routine, only to stuff his fat face in the kitchen.

SPAM is now the focus of young Judy's deadly mental powers.

The sparkles defeat Judy's demented psyche! Good wins over evil!

Judy is returned to normal, and now has a beautiful SPAM sandwich.

This cheese is so stringy! But I'm going to keep eating it because I'm afraid of the sparkles.

Oh no! The sparkles are back again.

Hooray! The sparkles brought us food, just like before. But now it is a different dish. Is there no end to the versatility of SPAM?

IT'S A SPAM WORLD AFTER ALL

It's easy to understand why millions of people around the world love SPAM. It is so delicious, it will hypnotize you into a lifetime of servitude. It just makes sense. What's hard to understand is just how BIG the world is. It's like, really, really, really big. But despite the hugeness of our world, SPAM has filled darn near every nook and cranny of it—12 ounces at a time.

To satisfy the enormous worldwide demand for SPAM, several plants churn out can after can. Two in the U.S.: Austin, Minnesota, and Fremont, Nebraska. Three more in the Philippines, Denmark, and South Korea.

Worldwide admiration

Some say the worldwide success of SPAM is due to World War II. It is true, SPAM was sent around the globe because its portability and long life made sense for war-torn civilians. But check the calendar, buddy. World War II ended a LONG time ago, and SPAM is still going strong.

Others may say the reason SPAM is so popular with some island cultures has to do with being prepared for emergency situations. But do they have typhoons and power outages and dock strikes every day? Because that's how often they're eating SPAM. Case closed.

Don't forget Australia, the UK, China, Russia, and plenty of other enormous landmasses. They like SPAM so much that, to them, there is nothing funny about it. At least not like it is to some Americans. It's a great food, they like it, they eat millions of pounds (or kilograms) of it. No joke.

In Australia, SPAM comes out of the can counterclockwise.

When it's **SPAM**® you know it's ham.

AUSTRALIA

SPAM World Tour

Andorra	Cuba	Israel	Panama	Suriname
Anguilla	Czech Republic	Italy	Papua New Guinea	Swaziland
Antigua	Denmark	Jamaica	Paraguay	Sweden
Argentina	Dominica	Japan	Peru	Taiwan
Aruba	Dominican Republic	Kazakhstan	Philippines	Tajikistan
Australia	Ecuador	Korea (North)	Poland	Thailand
Austria	El Salvador	Korea (South)	Portugal	Tonga
Azerbaijan	Estonia	Kyrgyzstan	Puerto Rico	Transkei
Bahamas	Fiji	Latvia	Qatar	Trinidad & Tobago
Bahrain	France	Lesotho	Ras al-Khaimah	Turkey
Barbados	Georgia	Lithuania	Romania	Turkmenistan
Belarus	Germany	Macedonia	Russian Federation	Turks & Caicos Islands
Belize	Greece	Malawi	St. Christopher-Nevis	Ukraine
Benelux	Grenada	Malaysia	St. Lucia	United Arab Emirates
Bermuda	Guatemala	Malta	St. Vincent	United Kingdom
Bolivia	Guyana	Mexico	Samoa	Uruguay
Botswana	Haiti	Moldova	Singapore	Uzbekistan
Brazil	Honduras	Montserrat	Slovak Republic	Venezuela
Canada	Hong Kong	Myanmar	Slovenia	Vietnam
Cayman Islands	Hungary	Namibia	Solomon Islands	Yugoslavia
Chile	India	Netherlands Antilles	South Africa	Zambia
China	Indonesia	New Zealand	Spain	Zimbabwe
Columbia	Iran	Nicaragua		
Costa Rica	Ireland	Norway		
Croatia				

*There are 117 countries where SPAM is a
registered trademark. Even more places eat it.
But those can be lawless, savage places where
trademarks mean nothing. Like Greenland.*

How much do they eat?

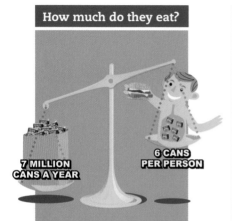

7 MILLION CANS A YEAR

6 CANS PER PERSON

Hawaii is pretty relaxed. They wear shorts and sandals to work. They often have Three Piña Colada lunches. But they have a voracious appetite for SPAM.

Hawaii

Hawaii, beautiful and mysterious, is first among Japanese businessmen looking for a boondoggle. It is the first choice of newlyweds. It is first in hula dancing, pineapples, and pure cane sugar. But most importantly, Hawaii is first in SPAM consumption.

Introduced to the islands during WWII, SPAM quickly became a part of Hawaiian society. Every self-respecting Hawaiian eats it. They say that SPAM is "ono." That means good. Fried SPAM and rice is a common meal for breakfast, lunch, or dinner. Fried wontons stuffed with SPAM and SPAM Saimin (a noodle dish with chunks of SPAM) are also frequent Hawaiian SPAM dishes.

SPAM is cooked up and served in practically every grocery store deli and convenience store. Countless restaurants feature SPAM dishes. In fact, every McDonald's in Hawaii has several SPAM items in their breakfast lineup.

McDonald's

Every one of McDonald's 75 Hawaii locations began serving SPAM for breakfast, just to see what the public reaction would be. Turns out they sold an average of over 3,000 SPAM items every morning. Of course, Hawaii isn't the only place McDonald's has started using SPAM. It's on the menu in many other places, including Guam, the Philippines, and Saipan. It's all part of the global plan for deliciousness.

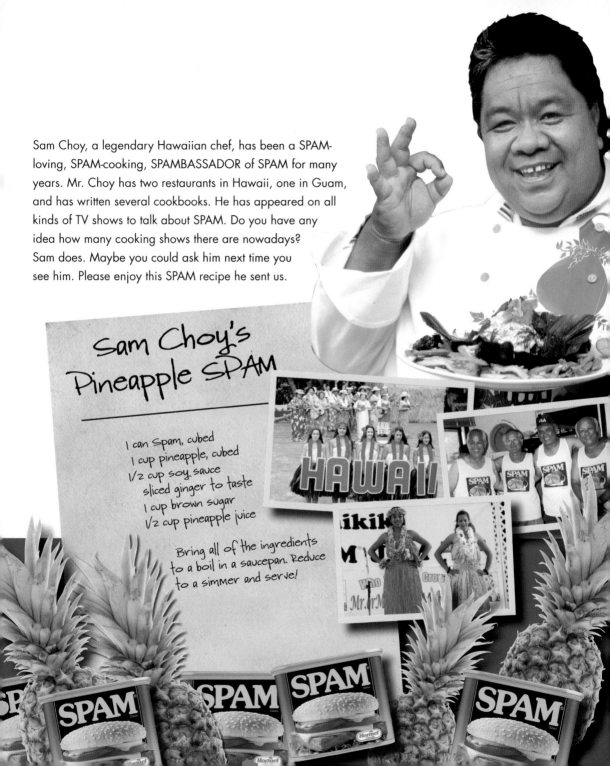

Sam Choy, a legendary Hawaiian chef, has been a SPAM-loving, SPAM-cooking, SPAMBASSADOR of SPAM for many years. Mr. Choy has two restaurants in Hawaii, one in Guam, and has written several cookbooks. He has appeared on all kinds of TV shows to talk about SPAM. Do you have any idea how many cooking shows there are nowadays? Sam does. Maybe you could ask him next time you see him. Please enjoy this SPAM recipe he sent us.

Sam Choy's Pineapple SPAM

1 can Spam, cubed
1 cup pineapple, cubed
1/2 cup soy sauce
sliced ginger to taste
1 cup brown sugar
1/2 cup pineapple juice

Bring all of the ingredients to a boil in a saucepan. Reduce to a simmer and serve!

SPAM fans are all over the world, from the forests to the seas, from the mountains to the grocery stores, from caressing polar bears to the majesty of conversion vans.

From can to my mouth
Is not fast enough for me
I need SPAM I.V.

Lamar's SPAM Haiku

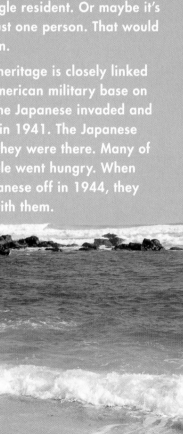

Guam

Guam likes SPAM. A lot. Their annual average consumption is about 16 cans per person. That's a whole lot of SPAM. It's over a can a month for every single resident. Or maybe it's like 5 cans a minute for just one person. That would be one heck of a SPAM fan.

Of course, Guam's SPAM heritage is closely linked to WWII. There was an American military base on Guam for decades, until the Japanese invaded and occupied the small island in 1941. The Japanese were not very nice while they were there. Many of the native Chamorro people went hungry. When American GIs ran the Japanese off in 1944, they brought plenty of SPAM with them.

How much do they eat?

2.5 MILLION CANS A YEAR

16 CANS PER PERSON

Did you know that Guam also has the highest density of snakes in the world? Just after WWII, cargo ships accidently transplanted the brown Treesnake there. Now they have no birds and over 13,000 snakes per square mile. We think it's true!

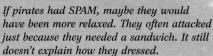

If pirates had SPAM, maybe they would have been more relaxed. They often attacked just because they needed a sandwich. It still doesn't explain how they dressed.

The GIs noticed how much the people of Guam loved SPAM, so they started to jokingly call it "Chamorro steak." Needless to say, SPAM has been a mainstay of the Guam culinary experience ever since.

Guam has its very own SPAM label, commemorating the liberation of Guam. There have been SPAM Olympics in Guam, where the best SPAM recipes from the island are sampled, critiqued, and awarded. SPAM is served at many restaurants, including McDonald's. The famous Hawaiian chef Sam Choy, renowned for his SPAM dishes, opened a restaurant there in June 1999. Not surprisingly, tourism is picking up.

I like to hear about Guam, but I don't know where it is. Please help.
—Jimmy, Phoenix, AZ
PS, Guam is fun to say.

Here's a map, Jimmy. Stay in school.

SPAM Musubi is an island favorite. Kind of like spilling beer on your wife-beater is a NASCAR favorite.

SPAM JAM is so wildly successful, they're already planning 87,000 more.

SPAM JAM Manila

The Philippines. You know, the country just south of Taiwan and very close to Malaysia? It's a deliciously tropical place with a very strong SPAM culture. Filipinos eat 3 million pounds of SPAM every year. That's over 8,000 pounds a day. Calculators don't lie, people.

But what is even more special about the Philippines is found in a mall. It is called SPAM JAM. It is the world's first SPAM restaurant. It is for real and it is growing. So get ready.

The grand opening in December 2003 was filled with Filipino celebrities. There were also models who looked like they came right out of a video game!

The menu is pretty much all SPAM. Yummers! There are also hot dogs available, but c'mon. Don't you know what they put in those things?

スパム ポーク&卵

スパムおにぎりの作り方

① 平らな面にノリを敷き胴型を図のように置きます。胴型の1/3まで、ごはんを入れ、かつおのふりかけを、全体にまぶします。

② 図の様に8～10ミリにスライスして焼いたスパムを2枚のせます。

④ 図の様に押さえ板と胴型をはずしてノリで軽く押します。

⑤ 押さえ板と胴型をはずしてノリを巻いて下さい。おいしいスパムおにぎりを好みの大きさに切って、ご使用下さい。

⑥ ●切り方の例
●Aタイプ（おにぎり大＝4個）ピクニック等のお弁当に
●Bタイプ（おにぎり小＝6個）オードブル等の詰め合わせに

●Aタイプ（おにぎり大＝4個）
2cm 2cm 2cm

●Bタイプ（おにぎり小＝6個）
2cm 2cm 2cm

Invited to a wedding in Southeast Asia? Give a SPAM gift pack. They regard SPAM as a fancy #1 luxury item. Sold in top stores for upwards of $45 U.S., these gift packs are exchanged for all kinds of reasons. Even instead of flowers on dates. Sexy!

참을수없는맛!
스팸
It's love at a first bite.

SPAM COOKING 101
SPAM MUSUBI

1. I say! Mrs. Bigglesworth, you seem not yourself today. Are you a bit peckish?

2. Then I say our tea party needs a little snack. Wouldn't you agree, Mr. Rinkytinkytoodles?

3. Don't worry, Mrs. Bigglesworth, I am quite adept at handling knives, as our time in Peru should have shown you.

4. Now we fry up the slices.
Do you know what it is I'm making for you?
It's a Hawaiian delicacy!

5. Now I pack the rice into the can of SPAM so
that it will be perfectly shaped for our SPAM Musubi.

6. Then I place the SPAM on top and wrap it up
with a strip of nori. That's Japanese for seaweed!

7. Isn't SPAM just the most delightful thing for our
friendly tea parties? This moment will last forever!

Alaska

In the land of igloos and yellow snow, there is a cozy SPAM oasis. Mr. Whitekeys' Fly By Night Club has worked hard to be the sleaziest bar in Spenard, Alaska, since 1980. Besides offering a menu filled with SPAM, the club features performances of The Whale Fat Follies, which involves a tap-dancing outhouse, whale blubber, and singing Eskimos. You can't blame Alaskans for having good taste.

Mr. Whitekeys is our SPAMBAS-SADOR of the North. His SPAM-FU is strong. His SPAM wall is mighty. His gaze is penetrating and knowing.

SPAM works better than a bear whisperer.

Legend has it that dogsledders bring it along on their trips over the ice and snow because it doesn't freeze. Sadly, this isn't true. SPAM does freeze. Hard as a rock. We've heard, however, that SPAM can be used to distract polar bears. They can pop open their SPAM and throw it at the bear. Not as a weapon, but as an inter-species offering of delicious peace.

They serve SPAM AND champagne!?! Get out of my dreams and into my mouth.

The Fly By Night Club does not actually endorse flying at night.

United Kingdom

The UK loves SPAM. Heck, anything even halfway delicious would score big there, compared to what they normally eat. After all, Scots eat haggis, which makes SPAM look like filet mignon. Not surprisingly, SPAM has been popular there since WWII, when it saved everyone's lives.

The English love to fry things. They may have perfected the technique with something called SPAM fritters. Basically, take your SPAM, dip it in some batter, and deep-fry it until the whole thing is crispy. Then douse it with vinegar so it's not so crispy. Then say "Cheerio! Rumpy, bumpy, pudding, pie! Would you care for a SPAM UP™, love?"

Don't tell the SPAMMOBILES, but there is a British sampling vehicle for SPAM, too! The main differences are the steering wheel is on the left and they drive it on the wrong side of the road. Also, they call trucks "lorries" instead of trucks. So we should call it the SPAMLORRY™. Sounds girly.

Keeping with the British tradition of Shakespeare, Charles Dickens, and Emily Brontë, these ads tend to be pretty boring.

SPAM with tongue? Are you tasting it, or is it tasting you?

FIND

THE

CAN

OF

SPAM.

The power of SPAM can move mountains. The flavor alone can cause earthquakes. The question is not how SPAM got up onto the mountaintop. It is how the mountaintop got underneath SPAM.

TAKING IT TO THE STREETS: THE SPAMMOBILE

The SPAMMOBILE is where the SPAM meets the road. This meaty machine is made of blue steel and burns rubber all across this land. It also brings free SPAM samples to all. It may be frightening to imagine the sharp dichotomy of something so wonderful yet so powerful. Don't be scared. Just think of it as a little baby. A little baby whose Daddy is a can of SPAM and whose Mommy is a monster truck. Cute!

No matter where you are in the parking lot, the eyes of the SPAMMOBILE burn deep into your soul.

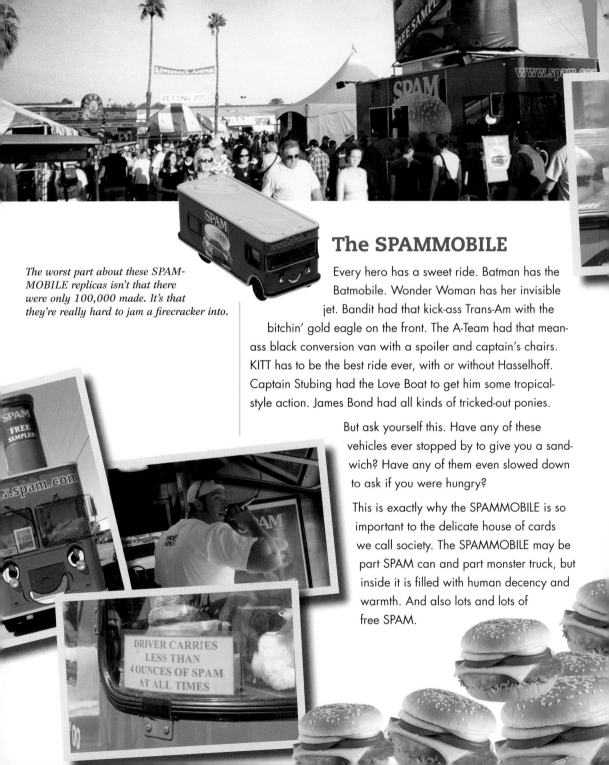

The worst part about these SPAM-MOBILE replicas isn't that there were only 100,000 made. It's that they're really hard to jam a firecracker into.

The SPAMMOBILE

Every hero has a sweet ride. Batman has the Batmobile. Wonder Woman has her invisible jet. Bandit had that kick-ass Trans-Am with the bitchin' gold eagle on the front. The A-Team had that mean-ass black conversion van with a spoiler and captain's chairs. KITT has to be the best ride ever, with or without Hasselhoff. Captain Stubing had the Love Boat to get him some tropical-style action. James Bond had all kinds of tricked-out ponies.

But ask yourself this. Have any of these vehicles ever stopped by to give you a sandwich? Have any of them even slowed down to ask if you were hungry?

This is exactly why the SPAMMOBILE is so important to the delicate house of cards we call society. The SPAMMOBILE may be part SPAM can and part monster truck, but inside it is filled with human decency and warmth. And also lots and lots of free SPAM.

DRIVER CARRIES LESS THAN 4 OUNCES OF SPAM AT ALL TIMES

Built from a trolley car chassis, the first SPAMMOBILE rolled out in 2001, followed by more and more. There is no telling how many are currently out there. As of this printing, the SPAMMOBILE vehicles have given out over 6.5 million samples. That means 6.5 million people are happier, more complete, and overall better human beings.

THE SPAMMOBILE SIDEKICK

EGG MAN

One day a horrible accident happened on the 101. And all the state troopers and all the L.A. Kings' men, couldn't put the Eggmobile back together again.

SAMPLES HANDED OUT

2002	2003	2004	2005	2006
856,000	1,037,000	1,344,000	1,506,000	1,713,000

FULFILL YOUR WILDEST DREAMS. DRIVE THE SPAMMOBILE!!!

Quick, find a scissors! Then run back here as fast as you can and start the rest of your life as a SPAMMOBILE driver. But don't just take sweet jumps and throw bitchin' parties all day. You need to feed people and protect the world from the meat-haters.

NOW WITH EASY-TO-FOLLOW DIRECTIONS!

1. Cut out SPAMMOBILE and desired accessories
2. Fold and play

Save the world with SPAM

Add a cape! or music! or drunken debauchery!

18+ section

Check the traffic with the SPAM copter.

Uncle SPAM!!

Hat are fur

fold

Do some bitchin' off-roadin'

Besides free samples of SPAM, visitors get free smiles! Then an awkward moment or two. Then back to smiles.

Each SPAMMOBILE is 28 feet long, 8 feet wide, and 10 feet high. For national security reasons, please make sure these blueprints don't get into the wrong hands. America is counting on you.

FINISH SCHEDULE
FLOOR: ALUMINUM TREADBRITE 100x48x192
CEILING: STUCCO ALUMINUM .032x48x96
WALLS: STUCCO ALUMINUM .032x48x96
STAINLESS STEEL 18 GA
COUNTER: STAINLESS STEEL 14 GA

NOTES:
1. INTERIOR LIGHT FIXTURES TO HAVE PLASTIC COVERS.
2. GENERATOR COMPARTMENT ACCESSED FROM EXTER

FLOOR PLAN

ENT LIST

ERATOR COMPARTMENT WITH
DUCT STORAGE ON TOP
DWICH GRILL QTY. OF 3
NLESS STEEL COUNTER
NLESS STEEL EXHAUST HOOD
SUPPRESSION SYSTEM
COMPARTMENT SINK
RY DOOR
OF ACCESS LADDER
ATED HOLDING CABINET
GLE DOOR UP-RIGHT REFRIGERATOR
ND SINK WITH SOAP AND TOWEL DISPENSER

13. 42" SERVICE WINDOW
14. NOT USED
15. ROOF MOUNTED A/C
16. FLUORESCENT LIGHT
17. CLOTHES CHANGING AREA
18. ELECTRICAL PANEL
19. WATER HEATER
20. ROOF ACCESS
21. BUN RACKS
22. PARTITION WALL BETWEEN SINKS
23. WASH DOWN HOSE BOX WITH HOSE
AND PISTOL GRIP NOZZLE
24. STORAGE AREA
25. CHEMICAL STORAGE COMPARTMENT

¿Dónde está el SPAMMOBILE?

Look at this map! It shows everywhere the SPAM-MOBILES have been. It's pretty much the whole darn country, isn't it? We could have just told you they went everywhere. But then what's the fun in that? Note to kids: Don't become book designers! The tedium of placing 800 little dots on a yellow map will turn you into a clock-tower sniper!

Hawaii

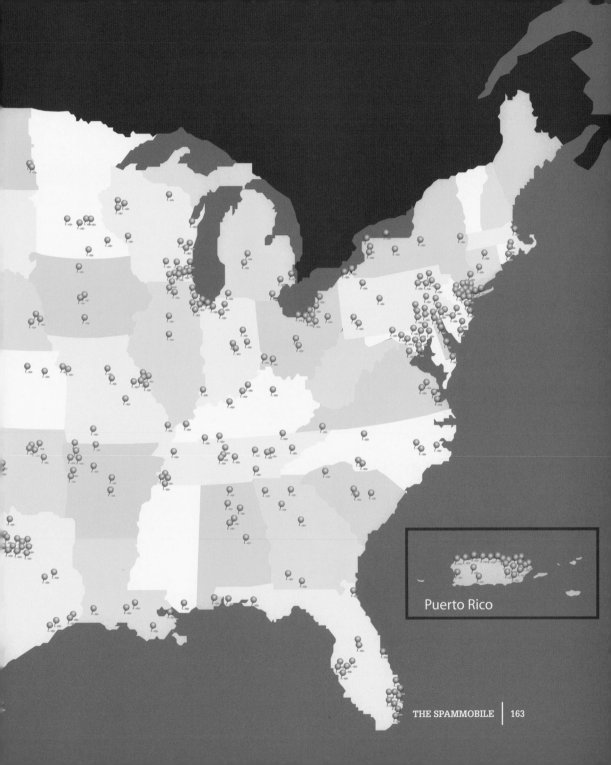

Puerto Rico

Whether you're being cute in snow, hanging with your girls, or visiting a Communist nation, bringing SPAM with you can make the hard times in life seem softer and saltier. Smile on, SPAM brothers and sisters! We shall overcome.

I HEART SPAM

Before you eat it
Just know that SPAM loves you more
Than other foods do.

Enrique's SPAM Haiku

Throwing a SPAM party is easy! But they can sure look like crap without professional photography and paid actors. Notice the perfect quadrillage grill pattern on the SPAM. This smacks of corporate intervention.

If you want to be a part of the junior SPAM dance team, you need to bring more than just jazz hands.

We 💗 the SPAMMOBILE!!

The life of the SPAMMOBILE driver is one of constant adoration. To see so many people express their love for SPAM, all across the country, must have a pleasant effect on one's psyche. Dock workers in Hawaii stopping to cheer the arrival of the SPAMMOBILE, crushing throngs of Puerto Rican SPAM fans, and a constant stream of one-bite SPAM conversions is enough to make you all pink and mushy inside.

They call the SPAM-giving window the "SPAMFESSIONAL" because it makes people tell their innermost SPAM secret. It's some pretty personal shit.

The SPAMMOBILE VS. The POPEMOBILE

We know what you're thinking. We can read your mind with secret technologies hidden inside this book. You're thinking, "Sure, the SPAMMOBILE is wicked cool. But it's no Popemobile." Think again, bucko! Here are the facts:

POPEMOBILE	SPAMMOBILE
4 metric tons (sounds exotic!)	Total weight depends on how much SPAM is inside
Over 20 in existence around the world	Classified
Made by VW, Fiat, Mercedes-Benz, Peugeot, Toyota	Made in U.S.A. U.S.A. U.S.A.!
Seats 2 + 1 pontiff with pointy hat	Seats 2, feeds millions
Donated to the Vatican by auto companies	Donated to the world by Hormel Foods
Spreads the good word	Spreads the good flavor
Boring papal white	Magical blue and yellow
Normal car size w/ a big dumb bubble in the back	28' long, 8' wide, 10' tall, with a 10' SPAM can on top! In your face!

SPAM JAM: THE GREATEST SPAM SHOW ON EARTH

So loved is SPAM by so many around the world that celebrating it just once a year seems trite. That's why there are several SPAM occasions held in separate locations. The three main events—in Minnesota, Hawaii, and Texas—bring in thousands of people every year. Many more unofficial and spontaneous SPAM celebrations could be going on as you read this.

It's fun to see the SPAM Queen, until she demands half of your food as tribute.

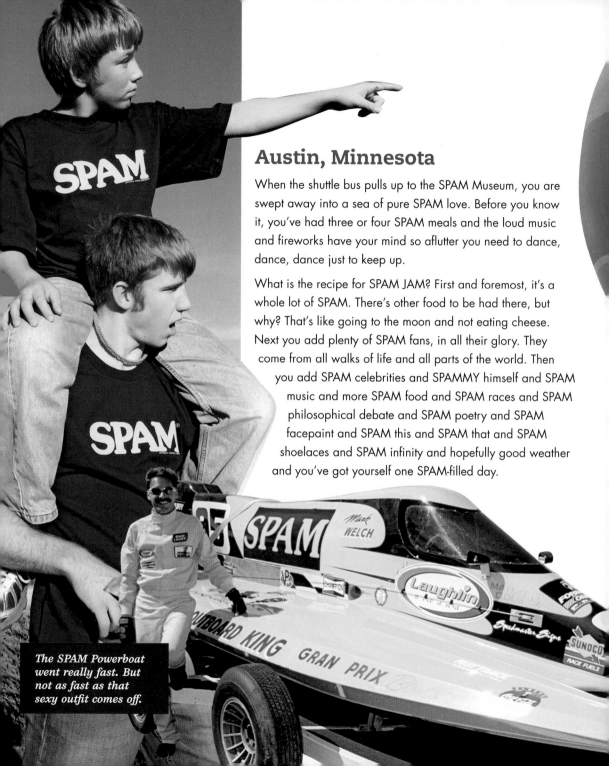

Austin, Minnesota

When the shuttle bus pulls up to the SPAM Museum, you are swept away into a sea of pure SPAM love. Before you know it, you've had three or four SPAM meals and the loud music and fireworks have your mind so aflutter you need to dance, dance, dance just to keep up.

What is the recipe for SPAM JAM? First and foremost, it's a whole lot of SPAM. There's other food to be had there, but why? That's like going to the moon and not eating cheese. Next you add plenty of SPAM fans, in all their glory. They come from all walks of life and all parts of the world. Then you add SPAM celebrities and SPAMMY himself and SPAM music and more SPAM food and SPAM races and SPAM philosophical debate and SPAM poetry and SPAM facepaint and SPAM this and SPAM that and SPAM shoelaces and SPAM infinity and hopefully good weather and you've got yourself one SPAM-filled day.

The SPAM Powerboat went really fast. But not as fast as that sexy outfit comes off.

Motorcycle gangs come from all across the country. Then they kick everyone's asses and take their women.

If you were a SPAM superhero, what would your special powers be?

Could you come up with new recipes in the blink of an eye? Would cold SPAM give you laser vision while fried SPAM gives you death-grip forearm-smash capabilities? Please write in your special power in the space provided:

_____

_____

Lots of weird stuff can happen when thousands of SPAM fans get together. SPAM weddings, SPAM car painting, SPAM waterskiing pyramids, SPAM singing groups, and so much more. But the weirdest thing of all is simply that thousands of SPAM fans get together.

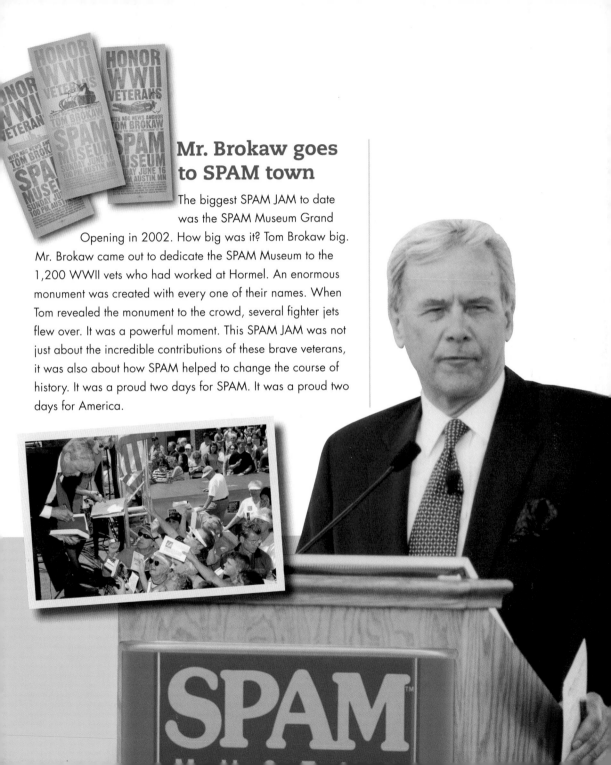

Mr. Brokaw goes to SPAM town

The biggest SPAM JAM to date was the SPAM Museum Grand Opening in 2002. How big was it? Tom Brokaw big. Mr. Brokaw came out to dedicate the SPAM Museum to the 1,200 WWII vets who had worked at Hormel. An enormous monument was created with every one of their names. When Tom revealed the monument to the crowd, several fighter jets flew over. It was a powerful moment. This SPAM JAM was not just about the incredible contributions of these brave veterans, it was also about how SPAM helped to change the course of history. It was a proud two days for SPAM. It was a proud two days for America.

If you're going to wear tights underneath your SPAM costume, make sure the cardboard is long enough to cover your bulges. Or match your underpants to your leggings. Just a suggestion.

SPAM ♥ BFF

When the robots come for us, keep your children safe with this SPAMBURGER disguise.

Nothing says corporate achievement like this SPAM jackalope. But it can also be a cry for help from your taxidermist.

Wearing a SPAM T-shirt on top of a mountain is cool. But toilet-papering it and running off is even cooler.

While festive, this SPAM poncho also sends a message to bears: Please rip me to shreds.

SPAM JAM, Waikiki

Over 20,000 SPAM fans come out to SPAM JAM on Waikiki Beach and enjoy all kinds of local SPAM favorites. The best chefs in Hawaii come out to show off their unique SPAM dishes. Free Hawaiian music stages are everywhere. Ukuleles are smashed at the end of every performance. And of course there's SPAM stuff for sale, T-shirts, flip-flops (they call them slippers in Hawaii), and everything else SPAM can put a logo on.

SPAM JAM Waikiki is home to the world's longest SPAM Musubi. It is well over 300 feet of meat. Like we weren't feeling self-conscious enough already.

SPAMARAMA, Texas

Held at the beginning of April in Austin, Texas, SPAMARAMA usually draws around 10,000 people for a day of SPAM music and SPAM events. It's the one day a year when Texans stop wondering about who shot J.R. and everybody gets their best duds on to raise a glass to the pink stuff they call "SPAYAM." There are two cooking events, one centered around how good the dish tastes, and another that is mainly about how creatively you play with your food. From mildly amusing to downright disgusting, these contestant concoctions always find a new angle on SPAM.

Everything's bigger in Texas. Except girls' shirts. Hooray for Texas!

These damn inflatable mascots should check IDs before giving SPAM hickeys. This girl could be 14 for all we know.

Throw your own
SPAM PARTY!

Throwing a SPAM party is a great way to find out who your friends really are. Unless that's why you already drink alone.

Clowns = good times. Period.

1.

OFFICE PARTY

Most prison cells are a spacious 7' by 12', but you spend your days in a tiny 5' by 5' cube watching for the "warden" and hiding your game of solitaire. It's time to have a SPAM office party.

"You know you deserve it"

Piñatas are racist and could spell a lawsuit.

Wear a really short skirt. It's not professional, but it will brighten everyone's spirits.

The basics

Inviting the office mime is often unavoidable. Put them in the corner and make them think they are trapped in a box.

Fun activities are important for any gathering. Think outside the box. Remember, management rewards creativity!

HALLOWEEN PARTY

Halloween has always been about ghouls and goblins, but now it can be about the spirits of dead pigs.

Don't be the only one without a SPAM costume! That's a beatin' fo' sho.

Costume 101

Take the stress out of finding a new costume by making it SPAM related!

"SPAM hors d'oeuvres."

"Hot SPAM 'n' eggs grilling on my face."

"SPAM on a Spatula."

Kids who don't wear SPAM costumes always get the Trick or Treat shaft.

Don't forget the games!

Bobbing for SPAM is super fun! It can also be done on the grill for an extra challenge.

A twist on a classic: Put cans of SPAM into empty pillowcases. Aim for the money-maker and swing away!

Race against your friends with giant chunks of meat in your mouth! Then after dark beat up kids for their candy.

SPAM Musubi costumes should not be worn around giant Hawaiians.

THE SPAM MUSEUM

For a time, leading scientists thought the Earth was the center of the universe. Then we all thought it was the sun, then it became popular to think that the universe was much, much bigger than we first suspected. Boy, did we all look stupid there for a while. As it turns out, the center of the universe is located at 1937 SPAM Boulevard, Austin, Minnesota.

In 2001 the SPAM Museum opens to the academic delight of meat historians across the globe.

the Spam MUS

In 2001, the SPAM Museum stopped being the dream of delicious dreamers and the subject of so many nightly prayers. A wholesome 16,500 square feet of pure SPAM knowledge, it is well worth the free admission. The exhibits within are numerous and plentiful, rich and memorable, with a side of "huh?"

Some lose themselves in the learning. Others have no recollection of their journey, it simply being too much for them to handle at once. But almost all visitors to the SPAM Museum come away with one over-riding thought: "It was better than I thought it was going to be."

700,000!!!

2003   2004   2005   2006

Over 700,000 visitors since the museum opened in 2001. That's like 100,000 times as many people that went to the last Cher concert!

"I got to see how they ground up the pigs at the same time as I was eating a delicious ground pig! Isn't America great?"

Minnesota

SPAM
MUSEUM
★

This map reveals every single interesting attraction in the state of Minnesota.

The radio station is a fake. The cans are empty. SPAMMY is just a statue. It makes me feel so alone.

SPAM™

SPAM TEST

Do you test positive for SPAM knowledge?
Take this quiz and find out. *NO urination required!

1. Match each item to the corresponding prison currency equivalent.

2. Where can you hide your SPAM?

a.  *b.*  *c.*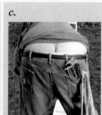

ANSWER: all of the above
If your SPAM is in danger, get it out of harm's way!

3. A ninja offers to slice your SPAM. Do you:

1. Tell him to cut it into a thousand slices in the blink of an eye.
2. Tell him to dice it Tiger Style.
3. Slam your door and hide in your bathtub.

ANSWER: 3
Never let a ninja into your home. Although less smelly than hippie invasions, a ninja-infested home will have broken lamps and all the furniture will be chopped to bits. Then you'd need to hire hit-mimes to quietly annoy the ninjas until they leave.

4. What type of cheese goes on a SPAM-BURGER?

a. American

b. provolone

c. Swiss

d. Jack

ANSWER: a
Of course it's American. What, are you some kind of Communist?

5. What's the best way to cook SPAM?

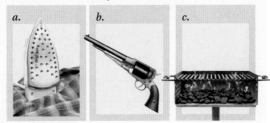

a.   b.   c.

ANSWER: c
While the other methods may be more readily available in your home, grilling offers the best flavor of the above options.

6. Find words. Now.

```
M O U S T A C H E P L F S
T U M I P E C L G O K A N
E N E N C A P M N R N C O
A I R C O P M U O K U I W
B C K E U S T R O C C A B
A O I T G M S D D H K L A
G R N S A Q W E L O L M L
X N K U R K F R E S E F L
S W L O I B T R I O Q W C
J D U M X Z Q U K U U F D
K O A C V T R E U O P J L
U Y T E R R T U O D B F H
```

7. Circle if it's appropriate for an empty can of SPAM.

vase ✓ X

neck brace ✓ X

best friend ✓ X

urn ✓ X

ANSWER: none of the above
Without the pink perfection, nothing in life is worth doing.

CAGEMATCH of Cute

8. In the cagematch of cute, who wins? Remember, only one can win. The others must die.

a.   b.   c.

ANSWER: b
Kitten = cute. SPAMMY = cute. Puppy = cute. Puppy in a Santa hat? Total cuddle city! Oooooh. I wuv it, I wuv it, I wuv it!

Getting your picture taken with things is an American pastime. "Look where I was this one time!" Yeah, we get it. You went somewhere. Hooray for you. Now put your little snapshot back in your wallet and hand me a towel.

Eternally frozen in white plaster, this apparently important moment in meat-packing history comes with its own audio re-creation. Seems weird they couldn't just cryogenically freeze their heads like other normal companies.

Memorizing propaganda literature and watching SPAM re-education films is mandatory.

Kids! What wonderful art comes from the innocence of childhood. Well, sometimes. We could totally draw better than this, but we were going for the cute factor on this page. Cute, cute, cute!

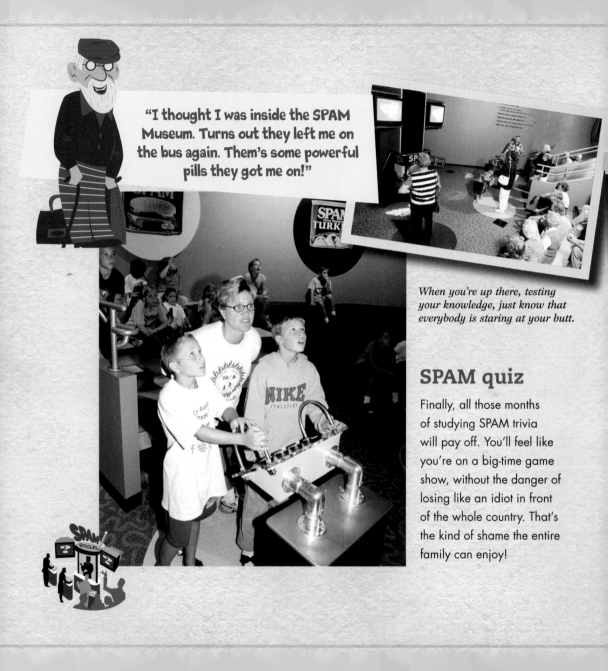

"I thought I was inside the SPAM Museum. Turns out they left me on the bus again. Them's some powerful pills they got me on!"

When you're up there, testing your knowledge, just know that everybody is staring at your butt.

SPAM quiz

Finally, all those months of studying SPAM trivia will pay off. You'll feel like you're on a big-time game show, without the danger of losing like an idiot in front of the whole country. That's the kind of shame the entire family can enjoy!

This exhibit offers the only legal way to give kids the feeling of just how fun child labor can be.

Assembly line

For those whose reading skills are decidedly lacking (I'm talking to you, kids!), there are hands-on activities. The simulated manual labor of making SPAM is good for children to experience, as is wearing a hairnet under a hard hat.

Learning all the gory details of hog processing is a birthday party to remember!

"I was on my way to Sturgis when I saw the signs for the SPAM Museum! I didn't see any naked, tattooed debauchery, but it was a relaxing time for my liver."

SPAM COOKING 101
BARRRRIED TREASURE

1. Arrr, mateys! Me innards are bare,
and methinks dinnertime is nigh.

2. Boil yer curly noodles in a steaming cauldron,
and drain said noodles of all their briny water.

3. Cube up a can of the almighty SPAM.
Chopping it to wee bits is a pleasure.

4. Avast! Now is the time to apply the cheesy mixture and yer cubes of pink.

5. Be stirring it up like ye means it! Put yer backs into it, boys! Or there'll be no food for the lot of you scurvy bastards.

6. Convey the prepared booty into a treasure chest of your liking. Be sure to hides it good.

7. Enjoy at yerrrrr own leisure. As it pleases ye. Arrrrr for now!

Sadly, these were the only cans these boys got to squeeze on Spring Break.

If you thought their SPAM cheers were awesome, you should check out their annual SPAM car wash.

Finally, photographic evidence that cats can cook. Read all about it in this month's CAT FANCY!

I want to be a SPAM fan
But I simply don't know how.
Do I have to learn a handshake
Or am I one right now?
Is it just inside me?
Or should I wear a sign?
Should I get a tattoo,
Or is the way I am just fine?
"Woe is me, woe is me"
I look to the sky and shout!
I wish there was a book to read
So I could find this out.
A reasonably priced one
With lots of fancy graphs
And some charts and pictures
To show me when to laugh.
Then I'd be a SPAM fan
Of that I am so sure
I'd be the best one I could be
My SPAM love burning pure.
The End.

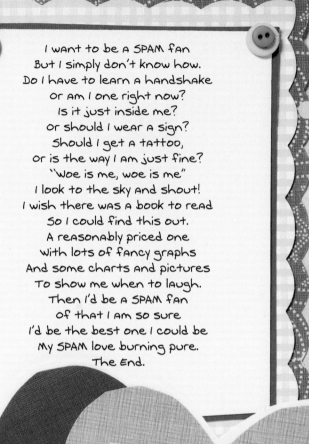

Yea! Short-shorts!

Green Midget Café

The famous Monty Python "SPAM" sketch set in the Green Midget Café is played in a replica of the Green Midget Café. Railings are available for the instant vertigo effect that will undoubtedly occur.

Dear Spam Mueseum,
          I thought that you could make the tour a little more exiting, otherwise it was great. I really liked the movie.

From,
Tyler

Children are often brutally honest. Children are often brutally stupid, too. Take that, Tyler. Maybe the tour would have been more exciting to you if it was built in a trailer home.

SPAM Shoppe

Nothing says trip to a meat-processing plant like a neon-orange camouflage hunting hat. There is no shortage of swag. From salt shakers emblazoned with the SPAM logo to flip-flops that leave the SPAM logo as your trail, anything with a printable surface is fair game. Think of that next time you try and be content with an ordinary clock!

"I always used sports enthusiasm and business trips to avoid my family. I never knew I could also use the SPAM Museum for that, too!"

IT'S TIME FOR SPAM

11 12 1
10   2
9   3
8   4
7   6   5

THE ORIGINAL SPAM LUNCHEON MEAT

Spam Football $10

SPAM

SPAM EST. 1937

SPAM® Museum established 2001

Austin, Minn

SPAMMY

I pledge allegiance to the SPAM.
And the entire SPAM family of products,
And to the flavor for which it stands,
Undefinable, but wicked awesome,
With hope there's enough SPAM for all.

Clip this out and place it somewhere close to your heart. In your office.
Next to your favorite plant. On the door to your peep-show room. On the
bottom of your cellmate's bunk. See this and repeat it to yourself every day.
Because you're a SPAM fan, and you should never be allowed to forget it.

Illustration & photo credits

Key:
HF = Hormel Foods, LLC
ISP = istockphoto.com
DB = Dustin Black

Chapter 1

8: reaching hands: DB. 10: bumper sticker: HF; motorcycle: HF; SPAM on board: HF; license plate: HF; patch: HF; slot machines: courtesy of IGT; Trivial Pursuit card: Trivial Pursuit® and related proprietary rights are owned by Horn Abbot Ltd. Used with Permission. 11: Uncle SPAM: Alyssa Greening. 12: tree: AbleStock. 14: quilt: Lyda Mandler, HF; car: Kenneth Szczesny, HF; SPAM queen: HF; hug: DB. 15: eye: Christy Kosmicki; singer: Simon Oxley, ISP; background: photo by Curtis Johnson; Dad's hippee tees photo: DB.

Chapter 2

16: tree: Art-Y, ISP. 18: ad: HF; SPAMINAL: Linda Black. 19: girl photo: AbleStock; unicorn illustration: Greg Paprocki. 20: Squeals: HF; can: HF. 21: shadow art of animals: Nova Art Explosion. 22: pig: DB; conveyer illustration: DB. 23: SPAM: HF; can: HF. 24–25: pig dream art: DB. 26: girl: pascalgenest, ISP; SPAM: HF. 27: oven art: ybmd, ISP & DB & HF; monkey: Kirza, ISP; table: llandrea, ISP; hinge: infospeed, ISP; boy: Anita Patterson, ISP. 28: teacher pig: bratan007, ISP; potatoes: pjmorley, ISP; folder: spxChrome, ISP; syringe: RussellTatedotCom, ISP. 29: SPAM: HF; girl: pascalgenest, ISP. 30: SPAMon: JoAnn Mapson; frame: Norman Scott, HF; left center: Donald Davis, HF; singer: Simon Oxley, ISP; background: photo by Curtis Johnson. 31: runner: Robin Duffy, HF; pigs: Dennis, HF; wedding: courtesy of NM. 32–33: SPAM food: HF; pig illustrations: DB. 34–35: Zippy: RussellTatedotCom, ISP. 36–37: guide: Alyssa Greening.

Chapter 3

38–39: opening chapter art: mstay, ISP & DB. 40: cave wall: AbleStock; dinosaur: LindaMarieB, ISP; caveman: cpuga, ISP; berries: AbleStock; grave: AbleStock; Ug and wife: HF. 41: boar: AngelIce, ISP; cat: Hughhamilton, ISP; pyramids: AbleStock; hieroglyphics: AbleStock. 42: pot art: DB; stained glass: AbleStock; teens: HF. 43: SPAM & Rillettes: HF. 44: elephant: RussellTatedotCom, ISP; tug boat: RussellTatedotCom, ISP; dog: TiffanyHinnen, ISP; leprechaun: RussellTatedotCom, ISP. 44–45: cacti: RussellTatedotCom, ISP. 45: clown: Mark Stay, ISP; marquee: SilkenOne, ISP; alien: Mark Stay, ISP; UFO: RussellTatedotCom, ISP; SPAM plant: RussellTatedotCom, ISP. 46: portable hog farm: Mark Stay, ISP; Napoleon: Wikimedia Commons; can history: DB. 47: Appert: Mary Evans Picture Library; book: dem10, ISP; mansion: photocay, ISP. 48: man: PhotoVic, ISP; salting meat: HF. 49: cart: AbleStock; soldiers: Alyssa Greening. 50: Parry: National Archives of Canada; can: Science & Society Picture Library; Prince Albert: NYPL Digital Gallery; chimney: stevegeer, ISP; scratched portrait: WPChambers, ISP; girl in car: WPChambers, ISP; cans: LuMaxArt2D, ISP. 51: tin can opener: OlgaLIS, ISP; key can: wolv, ISP; pull top: duckycards, ISP; 1st woman: andipantz, ISP; 2nd woman: andipantz, ISP; 3rd woman: forgiss, ISP; 4th woman: iconogenic, ISP. 52–53: Civil War: Library of Congress Prints and Photographs Division, Washington, D.C. 20540.

Chapter 4

54–55: houses: Art-Y, ISP. 56–57: pigs and blimps: Zuki, ISP & DB. 57: soldier: Alyssa Greening. 58–59: historical images: HF; cans: HF; ledger: HF. 60–61: illustration by DB. 62: New Year's: Alyssa Greening. 63: gramophone: Stouffer, ISP. 64: Daigneau: HF. 65: dollar: PIKSEL, ISP; dove: cyrop, ISP; outline: blackred, ISP; gold chain: DB.

Chapter 5

66–67: parachutes with SPAM: sx70, ISP & DB. 68–71: U.S. Army Corps Photos; Murrow: Hulton Archive/Stringer. 71: "Go Without" war ad: U.S. Army Corps; Margaret Thatcher: HF. 72: SPAMMY art; HF. New York Times cover: Reprinted by permission of the New York Times. 73: badge: HF; Khrushchev: HF; book illustration: DB; line: HF. 74–75: SPAMville: U.S. Army Corps Photos. 76: zero: Jack Copeland. 77: comics: Yank, The Army Weekly. 78–79: U.S. Army Corps Photos; comics: Yank, The Army Weekly; ad: HF. 80: misc. furniture: pronesis, ISP. 82: magazine cover: U.S. Army Corps. 82–83: U.S. Army Corps Photos. 83: Eisenhower letter and photo: HF. 84–85: girl scout: DB. 86–87: dog and fireplace art: phfft, prawny, ISP & DB.

Special thanks to our agent Laurie Abkemeier, our editor Suzanne O'Neill, Kevin Jones, Kara Mallory, Nick Meyer, Scott Aakre, Paul Krapf, Sven Neufeldt, Dan Goldman, Bob Pepper, Scott Ramlo, Sherry Andersen, Shawn Radford, Joan Hanson, the innovators at Hormel Foods, Mary Winter, Sarah Brown, Bryan Ojala, Denny Haley, Monica Hazelwood, Alex Berglund, Joanna Jahn, Cory Tobin, Clint Runge, Tyler Riewer, Jan Gura, Kelly Schulte, Brian Callamare and all the dedicated SPAMMOBILE drivers, Jack "the Stallion" Copeland, the estate of Nicolas Appert, Karen Winpenny, Mr. Whitekeys, Greg Paprocki, Alyssa Greening, Luke Hillestad, Christy Kosmicki, Brianna Smith, Zeke Elwood, Emily Barnhill, Curtis Johnson, Sam Choy, Tony Saucier, the limitless patience and constant support of Mimi and Tara, our families, our friends, our pets, and our beautiful computers.

. . . and most importantly, the billions and billions of delicious pigs.
Without them, this book never would have been possible.

xoxo

D&D